VOLUME III

SEASONS
OF THE
LORD

Bible-centered Devotions on

Fulfillment
and
Splendor

HARPER JUBILEE BOOKS

VOLUME III

SEASONS OF THE LORD

Bible-centered Devotions on

Fulfillment
and
Splendor

HERBERT LOCKYER

HARPER & ROW, PUBLISHERS

New York, Hagerstown, San Francisco, London

FIRST EDITION

A HARPER JUBILEE GIANT ORIGINAL

Designed by Eve Kirch Callahan

Library of Congress Cataloging in Publication Data

Lockyer, Herbert.
  Seasons of the Lord.
  (Harper jubilee books; HJG 02-05)
  CONTENTS: v. 1. Bible-centered devotions on purity and hope.—v. 2. Bible-centered devotions on resurrection and glory.—v. 3. Bible-centered devotions on fulfillment and splendor. [etc.]
  1. Bible—Meditations—Collected works.
I. Title.
BS483.5.L6   242'.08   76-9998
ISBN: 0-06-065267-5

77 78 79 80 81 8 7 6 5 4 3 2 1

Contents

Beauty and Bounty

Preface

Continuing our journey around the circle of the year, we find ourselves in the last half when summer reaches its fulfillment and brings us to the season *par excellence*. For lovers of flowers and fruit, July is a paradise. What a perfect month it is with all its glory and splendor! The seventh month suggests perfection, a virtue it displays. In summertime Jesus drew attention to a nearby field profuse with lilies and preached a powerful sermon on God's concern for us in all things.

Entering the loveliest time of the year, we discover so much pleasing to the eye. What better month is there for holidays when the problems of the rest of the year seem to fade? Farmers too hail this month of fulfillment with its rich harvest of golden grain and ripe fruit. Reaping what we have sown also reminds us that whatever we sow in conduct and character we will surely harvest, if not in time, then in eternity.

The golden year climaxes in the month of golden sun, golden leaves, and the golden harvest moon. What can compare to the glorious rainbow hues and satisfying sense of fullness and beauty September brings? How eloquent it is of the serenity of an accomplished destiny! Yet it is the month of shortening days and lengthening nights, reminding us of our gradual decay and likewise of God who is the length of our days.

x

FULFILLMENT
and
SPLENDOR

I sing of brooks, of blossoms and
   of bowers
. . . and July flowers.

      —Robert Herrick,
        "Argument of His Book"

A Portion of the Eternal

"The Lord is my portion, saith my soul, therefore will I hope in him." *Lamentations 3:24.*

In the Old Testament God is frequently referred to as the *portion* of his people. Since the word *portion* means "share," how privileged the saints are to have a share of, and in, God, or to adopt Shelley's phrase, "A portion of the eternal." The surprising thing is that God condescends to call his people *his portion.* "The Lord's portion is his people" (Deut. 32:9; Zech. 2:12). But he does not have a share in them; *he owns them.* They are his redemption right, and all who own him as their portion must recognize his claim to the sovereignty of their lives.

Courageous Chrysostom, church father of the fourth century, was not ashamed to tell the Roman emperor that there was nothing he could do to harm him since God was his portion. The pagan monarch replied, "I will take your riches."

"My treasure is in Heaven," the fearless saint answered.

"I will banish you from your friends," the ruler threatened.

"My best Friend will never leave me," Chrysostom replied.

"I will exile you from your country," the emperor said.

"Heaven is my Fatherland: Heaven is my home," was the church leader's ready answer.

Last of all, the godless emperor said, "I will take away your life."

The dauntless warrior met the threat boldly: "My life is hid with Christ in God. There is nothing you can do to hurt me."

If we believe that God is our portion, then let us by faith appropriate all we have in him. A. H. Waring wrote:

> My heart is resting on my God,
> I will give thanks and sing.
> My heart is at the secret source
> Of every precious thing.

Light a Candle, and Sweep the House

"I will search Jerusalem with candles." *Zephaniah 1:12.*

The unexamined life is not only fruitless but fatal. This is why the Bible presents the divine and human side of the examination of the human heart. Paul stressed self-*examination.* "Let a man examine himself." "Examine yourselves whether ye be *in* the faith" (1 Cor. 11:28). It is sadly possible for a person to work for the faith and yet not be *in* the faith. Therefore, such a search is imperative for the soul's eternal welfare.

Psalmists, however, stress the divine side of the search. "Lord, thou hast searched me out—or through and through" (Ps. 139:1). "Examine me, O Lord" (Ps. 26:2). Searching with candles intimates the minuteness of the heavenly searcher of hearts. Nothing must be left in the corners of one's life. A proverb has it, "Take heed you find not that you do not seek." When we work with God in the thorough examination of our hearts, we often discover those forbidden things we did not seek.

Are we prepared to examine ourselves carefully, deliberately, and prayerfully, taking God's Word for our rule and guide? Do we pause and look within to discover whether we are growing in grace or declining spiritually, whether we are being daily quickened by the Spirit, whether the love of God is being shed abroad in our hearts, whether we possess the evidence to prove the reality of our profession of faith in Christ? The psalmist prayed to be searched to see if there were any wicked way in him. Is this our daily prayer? We have no need to fear what the search may reveal, for what the candles bring to light of a forbidden nature the Holy Spirit can remove. Joseph Morris in "Poems of Inspiration" wrote:

> *Searcher of hearts! oh, search me still:*
> *The secrets of my soul reveal:*
> *My fears remove: let me appear*
> *To God and my own conscience clear.*

I Have Learned to Be Content

"Be content with such things as ye have." *Hebrews 13:5.*

How apt and appealing are the lines on the virtue of sweet contentment in John Bunyan's *Pilgrim's Progress*:

> *I am content with what I have,*
> *Little be it, or much:*
> *And, Lord, contentment still I crave,*
> *Because Thou savest such.*

Bunyan went on to describe how it is best for those on pilgrimage to have

> *Here little, and hereafter bliss,*
> *Is best from age to age.*

Baron Houghton, poet of the nineteenth century, could write of "the land of lost content." Do we not live in such a land? Is not discontent the most conspicuous feature of the multitudes around who are bent on seeking out some new thing? In our industrial world we forget the biblical declaration, "Be content with your wages." We may not have what we wish, but if we are the Lord's, we certainly have what he thinks best for us, and such godliness ever breeds contentment. We find it hard to learn Paul's lesson, "I have learned, in whatsoever state I am, therewith to be content" (Phil. 4:11). Several poets have followed Thomas Dekker of the early seventeenth century in writing of "Sweet Content":

> *Art thou poor, yet hast thou golden slumbers?*
> *Oh sweet content!*
> *Art thou rich, yet is thy mind perplexed?*
> *Oh punishment!*

With Christ as their abiding companion all believers should manifest such content, for he has promised to meet their needs. Grass grows content through the heat and the cold. Does not the old Book tell us that godliness with contentment is great gain?

The Secret Sympathy

"In all points . . . like as we are." *Hebrews 4:15.*

The word *sympathy* is not in the Bible, but all that it represents is. Are you not told that Jesus is "touched with the feeling of our infirmities" (Heb. 4:15)? The gospel hymn speaks of him as "the sympathizing Jesus." Walter Scott in "The Lay of the Last Minstrel" embodied such fellow feeling:

> *The secret sympathy,*
> *The silver link, the silken tie,*
> *Which heart to heart, and mind,*
> *In body and in soul can bind.*

When Jesus became man, he forged a "silver link" with humanity and came to know for himself its sorrows, temptations, and needs. Often we confuse *sympathy* with *sorrow*. But you can have genuine sorrow for a person afflicted in some way or another without experiencing personally the anguish he or she may be bearing. You cannot have sympathy for the person, however, if you have never known in your own heart what he or she is enduring.

The word *sympathy* implies an affinity or relationship, a correlation, the capacity of entering into and sharing the feelings, interests, and trials of others. The prophet Ezekiel said, "I sat where they sat" (3:15), implying that he shared the captivity of those around him. This fellow feeling makes us wondrous kind and is what Shakespeare had in mind when he wrote in *Troilus and Cressida*, "One touch of nature makes the whole world kin." Because Jesus became acquainted with our grief, he is able to help us in *our* grief. He enables us to learn life's secrets in the school of experience and then uses us in the world of tears to weep with those who weep and help them dry their tears. There would be fewer broken hearts around if only more of the virtue of sympathy were shown.

The Fountain of All Goodness

"How great is thy goodness, which thou hast laid up."
Psalm 31:19.

The psalmist told us that God treasures up his great goodness. It is *laid* up, or kept in reserve, for those who fear him until they need it; then he graciously disburses it. Is this not what the farmer does when his harvests are golden—store them up for when they are required? So it is with the goodness of God which is not emptied out in heaps all at once for our appropriation.

One of the most blessed features of him who gives us so many rich things to enjoy is that he never gives us in bulk all he has to bestow. It is impossible for him never to have more to give. "Have you received? Still there's more to follow," wrote P. B. Bliss in a hymn. Is it not encouraging to know that we never reach the limit in divine blessings? As J. R. Miller expressed it, "Every door that opens into a treasury of love shows another door into another treasury beyond. We need not fear that we shall ever come to the end of God's goodness, or any experience for which He will have no blessing ready." God's storehouses are always opened to us when we need the provision they contain. This is as true of nature as it is of grace, for when God created the world, he *laid up* in it supplies for every human need. Alas, how slow we are to learn that God's goodness is always found as need arises, as his many promises declare, "When thou passest through the waters, I *will be* with thee" (Isa. 43:2).

Once we find ourselves in the circle of need, we discover he is there to supply us with all that is necessary—a supply we often find in the valley of shadows. Bless God, the best of his goodness is *laid up* in heaven. This is why death for the Christian is far better, for then he is in the treasurehouse itself.

Boundless His Wealth As Wish Can Claim

"But thou art rich." Revelation 2:9.

The wealth of the believer that Jesus described is so different from the wretch depicted by Sir Walter Scott. The wretch, although "boundless his wealth," was "concentred all in self" and died "unwept, unhonour'd, and unsung"! The saints at Smyrna were materially poor yet rich. "I know thy . . . poverty," Jesus said, "but thou art rich" (Rev. 2:9). Broadly speaking, the majority of his followers are really poor in respect to what the world counts wealth, but he chooses the poor of this world, rich in faith, makes them heirs of his kingdom, and bestows upon them as much spiritual wealth as they wish to claim. An unidentified hymn writer said:

> *Call'd by grace, the sinner see,*
> *Rich though sunk in poverty;*
> *Rich in faith that God has given,*
> *He's a legal heir of Heaven.*

As poor sinners enriched by grace, we have *donated* wealth since Jesus has bequeathed us unsearchable riches. We likewise have the wealth of all the good things he has promised us. We are rich in relationships, having God as our Father, Jesus as our Savior and advocate, and the Holy Spirit as our invisible companion.

Because all who believe inherit all things, we should be rich in good works and rich in expectation, having before us the eternal city God is preparing for us. Our wealth is beyond compare, for his righteousness justifies us, his blood cleanses us, his Spirit sanctifies us, his angels minister unto us, and his heaven is to be our everlasting habitation. May grace be ours to claim our boundless wealth, here and now, and live as the heirs of God.

He's a Good Fellow, and 'Twill All Be Well

"It shall be well." 2 Kings 4:23.

Edward FitzGerald's portrait of one whose visage was daubed "with the smoke of Hell" but was yet encouraged to believe that all would be well with him since he was a "good fellow" illustrates the assertion of the Shunammite woman. Although she was a good person, as she set out on her journey to Elisha, she carried bitterness in her heart because of the death of her son. She came to experience that all is *well* to those who fear God, even when trials and sorrows are present.

It is always *well* with the righteous. When brought up against the fact of inherent corruption, all is well for you since you are not under the law but under grace. Sin cannot have victory over you. When you face the wiles of the Devil and are alarmed at his evil suggestions and subtle temptations, all is well. The God of peace is ever near to bruise Satan under your feet and to make you more than a conqueror. When your heart is cast down within you because of the trials, tears, and testings besetting your pathway, remember that *it shall be well.* Your Lord is at hand to cause all things, even the untoward experiences, to work together for your good. An unknown writer advised us to remember that:

Not a shaft can hit,
Till the God of love sees fit.

No matter what sorrows or separation overtake you, your lot is not singular but similar, for no testing can be yours that is not common to all. Further, because of his love and faithfulness God will not permit you to be tested and tried above that "ye are able." At all times let your exclamation be, "It shall be well," providing, of course, that it is well with your soul as far as God is concerned.

Then Heaven Make Me Poor

"The poor committeth himself unto thee." *Psalm 10:14.*

Ben Jonson of the sixteenth century coined the phrase, "When I mock poorness, then Heaven make me poor." When the psalmist referred to the perils of the poor (Ps. 10:9, 10), he doubtless had in mind impoverishment of means and ability to stand up to "the strong men," seeking their captivity. The *poorness* from which Ben Jonson sought to be free was a material poverty. Many of those who are denied earthly riches and appear friendless know what it is to have Jesus as their nearest friend to care for them. Jesus himself was poor, eating often at the table of others; yet he could rejoice in the friendship of those who ministered unto him of their substance.

Whether we are poor in substance or in spirit, may we be found ever committing ourselves unto him who is able to meet our very need. We must commit all to him, as debtors to him as our surety, as clients to him as our advocate, as those who are destitute to him as our rich and generous benefactor, as sinners to him as the Savior, as those who form the bride to him as the bridegroom. But why and how should we commit ourselves daily, deliberately, and unreservedly unto him? We commit ourselves

> To His grace, to be saved by it—
> To His power, to be kept by it—
> To His providence, to be fed by it—
> To His Word, to be ruled by it—
> To His care, to be preserved by it—
> To His arms at death, to be safely carried to Glory!

Committal to the Lord means that he will bring to pass all that concerns us for our present, spiritual good and for his glory.

A Double Blessing Is a Double Grace

"Thou shall be a blessing." *Genesis 12:2.*

We are not sure what Shakespeare actually meant when in *Hamlet* he wrote:

> *A double blessing is a double grace;*
> *Occasion smiles upon a second leave.*

What we do know, however, is that Abraham, as he answered the call of God to journey out into the unknown, received a "double blessing" which was indeed a "double grace." *I will be with thee . . . thou shalt be a blessing.* Being a blessing was contingent upon being blessed.

Unless ours is the continual dew of heaven's blessing, we cannot be a blessing to earth's needy. God cannot bless and use us above the level of our own spiritual experience. God's grace saves us, forms our characters, and fits us for service. By his wisdom he charts our course, imparts strength to accomplish his will, supplies all that is necessary to complete his design, and ultimately crown our efforts. He said, "I will bless *thee*," and how richly he does!

Blessed of him, we are a blessing to others by a meek and gentle spirit, by the imitation of the example of our Savior, by our intercession and service for the lost, and by our efforts to spread about by lip and literature the knowledge of the power of the Lord to save. Ours is a double grace, for both our salvation and service are of divine grace. Is your desire to be made a blessing since God has abundantly blessed you? If so, eternity alone will reveal all who have been blessed as the result of your fragrant life and consecrated service. Harper G. Smyth wrote:

> *Is your life a channel of blessing,*
> *Is the love of God flowing thro' you?*

A Graceless Zealot

"Come with me, and see my zeal for the Lord."
2 Kings 10:16.

Alexander Pope depicted those who fight for "modes of faith" as "graceless zealots," and Jehu was certainly *a graceless zealot*. He drove furiously, smote and did not spare, was consumed by ardent passion, and acted with speed and thoroughness as an instrument of divine judgment upon Ahab and upon Baalim. Although Jehu was carrying out the judgments of God, his own life was corrupt. We read that "he departed not from the sins of Jeroboam" and that "he took no heed to walk in the law of Jehovah" (2 Kings 10:31). Thus his zeal was not according to the knowledge of God's will, and his invitation to Jehonadab to accompany him on his ruthless mission revealed in a flash the central pride of his spirit.

How perilous is self-glorification in carrying out a divine mission! Jehu had zeal, but he was destitute of grace and of the passion to act only for the glory of God. Jehu was proud of his zeal, and such pride is always perilous, wherever it exists, since it leads to other personal evils. We manifest a perverted zeal when we strive to promote the cause of God by lack of tenderness toward others. Such graceless zeal is strange fire upon the altar, as Saul of Tarsus came to realize in his passion to destroy the church. There is a message for our hearts in Shakespeare's impressive lines in *King Henry VIII*:

> *Had I but serv'd my God with half the zeal*
> *I serv'd my king, he would not in mine age*
> *Have left me naked to mine enemies.*

God will never forsake us if we are consumed with a pure zeal for his house and glory and are always zealous of good works and of manifesting spiritual gifts.

14

O World Invisible, We View Thee

"Open his eyes, that he may see." *2 Kings 6:17.*

Francis Thompson, who gave us "The Hound of Heaven," also left us his appealing poem "The Kingdom of God." In it he affirmed the Christian's ability to see the invisible:

> *O world invisible, we view thee,*
> *O world intangible, we touch thee,*
> *O world unknowable, we know thee,*
> *In apprehensible, we clutch thee!*

Elisha's prayer for his young servant, when he was troubled about the visible hosts compassing the city of Dothan, was "Fear not: for they that be with us are more than they that be with them. . . . open his eyes, that he may see" (2 Kings 6:16, 17). The Lord opened the eyes of the young man, and he saw the "world invisible"—a mountain full of horses and chariots of fire round about Elisha. These enveloping hosts which ordinary eyes could not see filled the young man with fear, and his faith in "the king . . . invisible" was intensified.

Moses was able to endure manifold trials, for he saw him who is invisible. Is ours not the constant need to pray, "O Jehovah, open our eyes that we may see"? Invisible satanic foes surround us, and their antagonism and strength are great, often causing us to feel there is no way of escape from principalities and powers. The consciousness, however, that God's chariots of horses and fire are round about us delivers us from panic and despair and maintains our hearts in courage and in quietness, which is our strength. Such a faith is not the imagining of unreal sources of deliverance but the assurance that "invisible things are clearly seen" by those who constantly pray, "Lord, open thou my eyes, that I may see!"

Leave Nothing of Myself in Me

"Though I be nothing." *2 Corinthians 12:11.*

Richard Crashaw, who died in 1649, remains a star among godly poets. He penned this expression of his faith:

> *I sing the Name which none can say*
> *But touch'd with an interior ray.*

In his poem "The Flaming Heart" Crashaw confessed that his all was in Christ. He wrote:

> *Leave nothing of myself in me.*
> *Let me so read Thy life, that I*
> *Unto all life of mine may die!*

Paul's estimate of himself was that apart from Christ he was nothing but the chief of sinners and least of all the saints. Shakespeare's *Macbeth* says:

> *. . . nothing is*
> *But what is not.*

The apostle experienced such nothingness; yet destitute of "what is not," he abundantly possessed "what is," for he could say, "Having nothing and yet possessing all things" (2 Cor. 6:10). It may be humbling to our innate pride to sing, "Nothing in my hands I bring"; yet the only way up is down. We want to be *something*, but if we want God's best, we must realize that in his sight we are nothing and that all we need is in Christ. Nothing can come out of nothing, nothing can go back to nothing.

All we are is *by* Christ; all we have is *from* Christ; all we shall be is *through* Christ. Of ourselves we have nothing to boast. Are we willing to be nothing, even *scum* as Paul put it, that Christ may be all in all? The vision of his all-sufficiency destroys all pride of the flesh and brings us to the place where God can reveal his power.

Various Are the Tastes of Men

"Is there any taste in the white of an egg?" Job 6:6.

To gather together all the natural facts related in the Bible would make a most profitable volume. Here Job is asking about the white of an egg having any taste. What is the white of an egg? Well, an egg has two inner parts. The *yolk*, or yellow part, is the first section to be formed by the bird. The *white* surrounds the yolk and is a tasteless, odorless sort of jelly, made up mostly of water and known as *albumen*. The white is the chick's ration. As soon as the chick gets its beak, it pecks away at the white. By the time this is consumed, the chick is ready to leave its confined shell world for the larger world outside. Without this white of the egg the chick would die of starvation. Thus, although it has very little taste, the white is of great strength to the chick.

Reduced to abject poverty Job was forced to eat unsavory meats. He became so poor that he did not have a grain of salt to give a little taste to the white of an egg, now the choice dish on his table. Some of the most tasteless articles of food are the most profitable; yet they are despised because they do not appeal to the palate. This is also true in respect to spiritual food; those who lust after the flesh deem soul nutrition most distasteful.

The psalmist advised, "Taste and see that the Lord is good" (Ps. 34:8), and once the Lord is thoroughly tasted and appropriated, he becomes living food for our souls. Taste is something that can be cultivated. In spiritual things this is certainly so. If you have little taste for the Word, for prayer, for holiness, like the chick without the white of an egg, you will die of starvation. So do not be fastidious; eat and live!

The Mystery of Migration

"The stork in the heaven knoweth her appointed times."
Jeremiah 8:7.

The stork knows the time of her migration, and the dove, the crane, and the swallow observe the time of their return. The miracle of bird migration is a mystery and a striking evidence of the unsearchable greatness of the Lord. The ability of birds to fly to parts thousands of miles away and return home—often to nest in the very same house where they nested the year before—is one of the most marvelous yet strangest features in nature. Despite all the efforts of naturalists to explain how birds fly to warmer climes to obtain food and reproduce under the right conditions, we still do not know how they leave and return as they do or what signals and guideposts they note to direct them.

We believe that on the fifth day of creation, when God fashioned "fowl that may fly above the earth in the open firmament of heaven" (Gen. 1:20), he created the birds with a built-in instinct. He is thus responsible for their flight of thousands of uncharted miles over land and water.

At creation humankind was made with a built-in instinct for God. St. Augustine wrote, "Thou hast made us for Thyself, O Lord, and our hearts are restless until they rest in Thee." By his indwelling spirit, the same creative God guides and directs us through the days and years of our earthly sojourn to the land of pure delight which he is preparing for us. Our spiritual instinct tells us that our flight from this godless, blood-soaked earth is not far distant. The question is, Are we ready for our heavenly migration which is nearer than we may realize?

Men's Eyes Were Made to Look

"Any man, when he looked unto the serpent of brass,
he lived." *Numbers 21:9*, RV.

We are indebted to Shakespeare for the phrase in *Romeo and Juliet*, "Men's eyes were made to look, and let them gaze." The serpent-bitten Israelites of old put their eyes to good use when they looked and gazed upon the brazen serpent lifted up on a pole. There was, of course, no healing virtue in the metal serpent which Moses was commanded to make. Relief came through the look which indicated obedience to the divine edict, *Look and live!*

All who refused to look perished from the poisonous sting of the serpents which God sent upon the people as a punishment for their sin. But the remedy he provided was in the form of what he permitted for the disobedience of the people. Bitten by death-dealing serpents, they had to look at the brazen serpent if they wanted to live. As any man looked, he lived because in looking he bowed to the divine will and thus made it possible for God to restore and heal him. The *look* required was not to be a mere glance or "the only loveless look, the look with which you pass'd" that Coventry Patmos wrote about. The look of the dying Israelite indicated repentance for sin, longing to be free from the fire of poison, and faith in the remedy God had provided.

Jesus used the serpent lifted up on a pole as an illustration of himself. Made in the likeness of sinful man but without his sin, Jesus was lifted up on a tree for the sinner's restoration. And the divine command is, "Look unto me, and be saved." Bless God, there is life for a look at the crucified one! It is to be hoped, my friend, that you looked to him for salvation and that your gaze has never wandered from his face. We repeat with C. H. Spurgeon:

I looked at Him—He looked at me,
And we were one forever.

Memory, the Warder of the Brain

"Lest thou forget." Deuteronomy 4:9.

Shakespeare in *Macbeth* not only gave us the striking function of memory in the title of this meditation, but also phrases like "the table of my memory" and "the memory be green" (*Hamlet*). Evidently God desired his people to keep their memories green in respect to all he had accomplished for them. In *Kidnapped* Robert Louis Stevenson wrote, "I've a grand memory for forgetting, David."

With the Israelites of old we too have a "good forgettery" and need the constant plea of Scripture to remember the Lord and all his mercies. On more than one occasion Moses warned the people not to forget their spiritual ideal, for he knew that forgetfulness of the solemn and majestic manifestations they had witnessed would be a sin against God and evidence that their exalted privileges were not of great value.

How apt we are to forget the commands, the deliverances, the disciplines, and at times the very love of God! "Memory is a non-moral function of the soul," said Dr. G. Campbell Morgan, an English Bible teacher and preacher who died in 1945. "If it is either to help or hinder it must be trained and used. When it is employed to key certain facts in the mind, so that they may influence the will, it is one of the greatest forces for good. Memory serves us as an inspiration to true conduct." In his first inaugural address as president, Abraham Lincoln spoke of "the mystic chords of memory," influencing "the better angels of our nature." In *Recessional* Rudyard Kipling delineated the beneficial ministry of memory:

> *Lord God of Host, be with us yet.*
> *Lest we forget—lest we forget!*

I'll Put On My Considering Cap

"Consider how great things the Lord hath done for you."
1 Samuel 12:24.

With old John Fletcher, who died in 1625, we too have need to put on our "considering cap"—and keep it on! Scripture employs the word *consider*, which means "to look at attentively," almost one hundred times. A glance at these references reminds us who and what we are to consider and how consideration influences conduct. Samuel emphasized this latter aspect of consideration when, rehearsing the deliverances of Jehovah, he told the people that their constant consideration of the great things accomplished for them would incite them to "fear the Lord, and serve him in truth with all your heart" (1 Sam. 12:24).

Too often we consider our miseries and fail to count our mercies. Taking to our own hearts the constraining plea of Samuel to "consider how great things the Lord hath done," what else can we do but magnify him for the love that prompted him to surrender his beloved Son for our salvation. Consider how Christ himself never fails and never forsakes us and will remain with us until he perfects that which concerns us. Consider how he supplies us with all we need from day to day, corrects our mistakes, conquers our foes, withholds no good thing from us, and gives us his promises to plead. Consider the innumerable proofs of his faithfulness and, above all, the unmeasured marvel of his best treasure—*himself!*

When we consider all these things and many more, what else can we do but praise him for the past and pledge ourselves to trust him in the future, confident that, having blessed us, he will do still greater things for us. Is your considering cap well fixed upon your head? May God not have to say of us, "My people doth not consider" (Isa. 1:3).

But We, Like Sentries, Are Obliged to Stand

"As the Lord God of Israel liveth, before whom I stand."
1 Kings 17:1.

The standing sentries which John Dryden described in "Don Sebastian" stood "in starless nights, and wait the 'pointed hour." But when the appointed hour arrived for Elijah the Tishbite, he came, not only standing before the Lord, but daring to stand *up* for him in a most dramatic way as a courageous sentry until his chariot ride to heaven. In a startling way the prophet broke in on the national life of Israel. Like a bolt from the blue upon the prevailing spiritual darkness, he initiated a new method of divine rule, namely, prophetic ministry. From this point on the prophet was superior to the king in the kingdom of Israel. Elijah's very first message declared his God-given authority. He affirmed that Jehovah, Israel's God, lived and that the message he was about to deliver was direct from Jehobah's throne before which he stood.

Elijah challenged all earthly authority and swept aside human protection. He stood before the Lord, and he believed the Lord would stand up for him, which he did, protecting and providing for him in wonderful ways.

Paul exhibited the same fearless spirit as Elijah when he confessed, "God whose I am, and whom I serve" (Acts 27:23). God ever breaks in upon human history, as he did in Elijah and Paul, and in Martin Luther who also said, "Here I stand, I can do no other," and asserts his authority and displays his power. Men may refuse the message, and persecute the messenger: but the word he speaks is the word of Jehovah, and it is the word by which men live or die, according to their response to it. Are you standing before the Lord and the world as God's messenger, unafraid of your adversary the Devil?

The Secret Things Belong to God

"The Lord shall be thy confidence." *Proverbs 3:26.*

Scripture has much to say about our confidence in God and that in such confidence is strength; but in the verse before us Solomon spoke of God as our confidence, or *confidant.* He is a confidential friend or one to whom secrets are confided. As the friend sticking closer than a brother, his ears are ever open to hear the secrets of our hearts. The secret things about his children belong to him, are never repeated to others, and are forever locked up in his heart. What we tell him about ourselves in the secret place never travels beyond him because, being who he is, he cannot betray the trust of any child of his.

The margin of the New American Standard Bible reads, "The Lord will be *at your side,*" and this translation is apt, since the rest of the verse reads, "and will keep your feet from being caught." Thus our heavenly confidant is also our protector.

The word *confide* is from a Latin root meaning "to trust," and we confide in the Lord because we trust him. Our assurance is that he always listens sympathetically to all we have to tell him. God presents himself as being honorable, as the one to whom we can communicate all that concerns us, and as the one from whom we can receive wisdom, guidance, and peace. The promise is that if we trust him as our confidential friend we shall be as Mt. Zion which cannot be removed. Such is the marvel of divine grace that our heavenly confidant reciprocates by confiding in us. Has he not said that he will share his secret with us and reveal his covenant to us? "The secret of the Lord is with them that fear him" (Ps. 25:14).

To Sing of Time or Eternity

"The angel sware . . . that there should be time no longer."
Revelation 10:5, 6.

Tennyson described his fellow poet John Milton as "God-gifted organ-voice of England" and as one who was "Skilled to sing of Time or Eternity." Revelation, the final book of the Bible of which it has been said that without tears it was not written and without tears it cannot be understood, sings of both time and eternity, with emphasis upon the eternal blessedness of the redeemed. John wrote of the welcome oath and cheering promise of the angel concerning the ending of time and the commencement of eternity for the redeemed. Wordsworth would have us know the

Characters of the Great Apocalypse
The types and symbols of Eternity
Of first, and last, and midst, and without end.

Joseph Addison, English essayist and poet of the early seventeenth century, remarked, "Eternity! thou pleasing, dreadful thought!"

But whether we are to find eternity pleasing or dreadful depends upon our relationship to him who inhabited eternity. William Blake reminded us that

. . . He who kisses the joy as it flies
Lives in eternity's sunrise.

Is our joy of the Lord enabling us as pilgrims to eternity to live in its sunrise? The moment Christ calls us home, "there shall be delay no longer" for those redeemed by his precious blood. There will be nothing to dread as we forsake time and pass into eternity for union with the glorified and immortal saints of all ages already there. May we be found living as those ready for the end when time shall be no more.

The Continual Dew of Thy Blessing

"I will be as the dew unto Israel." *Hosea 14:5.*

Poets of all ages have extoled the virtues of "bespangling herb and tree." Tennyson, however, referred to a day when "there rained a ghastly dew." A fiat of divine judgment was, "Let there be no dew" (2 Sam. 1:21). For those living in the East, heavy dew was absolutely necessary since the earth depended upon it; hence, its significance in Scripture.

What dew is to fields and fruits, God offers to be to his redeemed people. As the dew cools and refreshes the dry, barren earth, so God waits to refresh our hearts with the assurance of his love and tokens of his favor. As the dew softens and breaks up the clods of the valley, so God softens and dissolves hard and impenitent hearts. As the dew prepares the ground for the seed and causes it to vegetate and grow, so God prepares hearts to receive his Word and causes it to bring forth fruit in our lives. As the dew falls insensibly and when it is most needed, namely, in the evening, so God comes to us when we need his quickening and fructifying operations.

By nature our hearts are dead and but for the grace of God cannot manifest life, beauty, or fruit. Regeneration by the Holy Spirit requires God's continual dew and the need to sing always, along with an unknown writer:

> Come, Holy Ghost, as heavenly dew,
>   My parchéd soul revive;
> The former mercies now renew,
>   Quicken and bid me live:
> Thy fertilizing power impart
> And sanctify my barren heart.

That Kiss, Which Is My Heaven to Have

"Let him kiss me, with the kisses of his mouth."
Song of Solomon 1:2.

Fundamentally, a kiss is an evident token of love or affection between two persons; symbolically it is intended to express the manifestation of love the Lord God has for his children. Said the Roman poet Catullus, who lived before Christ, "Kiss me a thousand times o'er." The spiritual mind can see in "the kisses of his mouth" the varied evidences of his boundless love for his beloved ones. Shakespeare had Cleopatra say of Antony's embrace, "That kiss, which is my heaven to have."

God's *kiss of reconciliation* was received in the moment of our surrender to his claims and meant heaven to us in a very real sense, just as the kiss of the father for his prodigal son meant installment in the father's home. God's *kiss of acceptance* is ever warm on our brow as our hearts are assured that we are his through grace alone. The *kiss of communion* is our daily enjoyment of his unfailing love; the lips of his blessing meet the lips of our asking.

Judas prostituted such a token of affection when he hailed his master with a kiss, not of love but of treachery, that resulted in his death. Previous kisses of his mouth, however, will be lost in his *kiss of consummation* when we finally meet him whom our hearts have loved. Richard Greene of the fifteenth century wrote of one, "My kisses are his daily feast." May the kisses of the mouth of our heavenly lover be our daily feast! The lines from "St. Paul" by the English poet F. W. H. Myers are impressive:

Moses on the mountain
Died by the kisses of the lips of God.

The Lord grant that each of us who have kissed the Son die thus. Surely there is no better way to die.

A Door to Which I Found No Key

"The Lord shut him in." *Genesis 7:16.*

Omar Khayyám said in the *Rubáiyát*:

> *There was the Door to which I found no Key;*
> *Here was a Veil through which I might not see:*

The door that shut Noah and his family in the ark had no key, for God shut them in. It is important to observe that when the hour came for those who were to be saved from the deluge, God did not say, "Go in," but "Come in." Such a request implies that he was already inside the ark and that he would remain with his servant and his family all through the flood. Once the ark rested on dry ground, he would open the door for them to enter a renewed world.

Doubtless many doors had been shut in Noah's face because of his unflinching faith in God and his Word, but such refusals mattered little now that God had opened a door of escape from death and then closed the door upon the world that had despised the testimony of his servant. The hand of divine love shut Noah and his family in the ark away from a wicked and condemned world.

How grateful we are that we responded to the divine call, "Come thou and all thy house into the ark" (Gen. 7:1), and that the door of electing purpose interposed between us and an evil world! It is blessed to know that we are shut in *with him* and enclosed in the same circle as the Holy Trinity. Outside the ark all was ruin, but the disastrous floods only lifted Noah nearer heaven, and all within the ark was rest and peace. Out of Christ, our ark, we perish. In him we are saved and safe, for as the door, he has no key, and once shut in with him, no man can open such a door. Are you on the right side of that door?

While Memory Holds a Seat

"We will remember thy love." *Song of Solomon 1:4.*

Lifting the following lines from Shakespeare's *Hamlet,* I link them to Solomon's affirmation:

> *. . . Remember thee?*
> *Ay, . . . while memory holds a seat*
> *In this distracted globe.*

Only our constant remembrance of the undying love of God for us can save us from being engulfed in our distracted globe. Wordsworth could write "that nature yet remembers" as a "perpetual benediction." Surely there is no theme so sweet and precious to God's children as that of the love of his heart fixed on them immutably and eternally. The Son of his love will not let us forget his love. Did he not institute his Supper that we might remember the matchless history of his love? Samuel Rutherford, seventeenth-century Scottish theologian, teacher, and writer, would often sigh, "Oh, for as much love as would go round about the earth, and over heaven—yea, the heaven of heavens, and ten thousand worlds—that I might let all out upon fair, fair, only fair Christ!"

If only we could give all the love in all pure hearts in one great mass, a gathering together of all loves to him who is love and altogether lovely, what a perpetual benediction would be ours. May grace be ours to remember his eternal love, to comfort our hearts amid changing friendships, to encourage our minds amid the gathering darkness in the world, to inspire us with fortitude in times of testing, to begat patience when we find ourselves burdened and oppressed, to reconcile our troubled minds under bereaving dispensations, and to produce and maintain zeal and devotedness in the Master's service. If we forget all else beside, let us remember his love and daily rest in it.

There's a Divinity That Shapes Our Ends

"Ye meant evil against me; but God meant it for good."
Genesis 50:20, RV.

Scripture and also personal experience confirm Shakespeare's dictum in *Hamlet* that

> *There's a divinity that shapes our ends,*
> *Rough-hew them how we will.*

With kind and tender words Joseph consoled his brothers who were fearful that he would punish them for their past treatment of him now that their father was dead. How assured they must have been of his love and favor! They heard him say that God had made use of their wicked action, when they sold him as a slave, in order to preserve the life of many people and to fulfill his plans concerning both Hebrews and Egyptians!

It is comforting to know that there are never any mistakes in the divine government. The blunders and failures of men are overruled and resolved into the perfect wisdom, might, and purpose of God. Religious leaders were bent on evil against the Lord Jesus and succeeded in crucifying him. A divinity was shaping the end of his agonies and death, and a vast, unnumbered multitude rejoices in the shed blood of the Redeemer. God is superb in making crooked things come out straight, and he can cause even the most unwelcome events of life to work together for our good. "*All* things come of thee" (1 Chron. 29:14). The words by Frederick W. Faber apply to that which Joseph came to experience, as saints in every age do:

> *Ill that He blesses is our good,*
> *And unblest good is ill:*
> *And all is right that seems most wrong,*
> *If it be His sweet will.*

The Greater Man, the Greater Courtesy

"Rabbi, where abidest Thou? He said, Come and ye shall see." *John 1:38–39*, RV.

Mother Julian of Norwich, a saint of long ago, loved to call Jesus "our courteous Lord." Speaking of prodigals returning to him, she said of his welcome to such wanderers, "Then showeth our courteous Lord Himself to the soul, with friendly, welcoming, saying sweetly thus: My darling, I am glad thou art come to Me; in all thy love I have been ever with thee; and now seest thou My loving." What a joy is ours when, at his courteous bidding, we come in faith to him!

We cannot read the above Scripture without seeing how courteously Jesus dealt with the two men who followed him after hearing John describe him. What sympathy and understanding Jesus revealed! Strangely drawn to him, the two travelers hardly dared to take the initiative of speaking, but Jesus turned to them in friendly inquiry, "What seek ye?" Enraptured by his kindness, all that they could say was, "Master, where dwellest thou?" (John 1:38). He did not rebuke them by answering, "That's no business of yours," but answered their unspoken desire with a sweet invitation, "Come, and ye shall see." And he took them home with him. We can imagine how those two men came to listen with growing wonder and deepening joy to his precious conversation.

This is always the manner of Jesus. What must be borne in mind is the fact that part of the same courtesy is seen in that he never thrusts himself upon us. So delicate is this courteous one, he will not enter where his company is not really desired. But how good and kind he is to those who seek him. Old Thomas Dekker wrote of him:

> *The best of men*
> *That e'er wore earth about Him, was a sufferer,*
> *A soft, meek, patient, humble tranquil spirit,*
> *The first true Gentleman that ever breath'd.*

The Footstool of the Virtues

"Be strong, and of a good courage," Joshua 1:6.

Writers and poets all down the ages have praised the excellencies of courage, whether physical, moral, or spiritual. Robert Louis Stevenson called it "the footstool of the virtues, on which they stand." In his rectoral address on courage given at St. Andrew's University, Scotland, in 1922, James Barrie said, "Courage is the thing. All goes if courage goes."

The Bible has a good deal to say about saints living courageously. In his last counsels to the people he had guided for forty years, Moses instructed them to "be strong, and of a good courage." His successor, Joshua, several times repeated the same exhortation as he commenced to lead the Hebrew nation. Joshua received the solemn charge from God to "be strong and of a good courage; be not afraid, neither be thou dismayed: for the Lord thy God is with thee" (Josh. 1:9). The courage he was to manifest was a mixture of the physical and spiritual.

Plato declared that the guardians of his ideal city should be men whose courage to defend the citadel was grounded in sound training in the true nature of the human spirit. The courage the Bible commands and commends is of the sort God himself inspires, and such courage "mounts with the occasion." Moral courage often transcends physical courage, and this is the brand we need to stand up for the cause of God and his righteousness in the face of a godless, hostile world. George Farquhar, the seventeenth-century dramatist, wrote:

> *Courage the highest gift, that scorns to bend*
> *To mean desires for a sordid end.*

John Milton asked for "courage never to submit or yield." We too may sing the words of an unknown writer: "Since I must fight if I would reign, increase my courage, Lord!"

A Joyous Exchange

"Thy statutes have been my songs in the house of my
pilgrimage." *Psalm 119:54.*

David, the sweet singer of Israel who has a good deal to say about singing, tells us where the substance of his songs came from: they were
all borrowed from the Word of God. It is amazing how many of our
hymns—ancient and modern—are founded upon different phrases of
Scripture. Commenting on David's exchange of statutes into songs,
Alexander Smellie said, "It seems strange that one should break into
melody and music over *statutes*, the enactments of the law and re-
straints of authority; for are not the imperatives *Thou shalt* and *Thou
shalt not* a curtailment of delight, a crippling of ambition, a checking of
impulse? Must I not be free, if my mouth is to be filled 'with laughter
and my tongue with singing?' But no! the commandments of God do not
really fetter; they introduce my soul to joy and peace."

Have we not abundant reason for making God's statutes our songs?
Scripture ends turmoil within and changes confusion into order. It
delivers one from the burden of guilt, from fear of the world, and from
the sting of death. Scripture sets eternity in the heart and guides into a
knowledge of a Savior outside ourselves and into a life of likeness to
him who died for our redemption on the cross.

David knew that the terms of the Law were not only melodious but
strictly prosaic and harsh; yet salvation and stability were secured to
the psalmist by that Law, and so he put it to music and sang of him
who had become his strength and deliverer. Not only did those statutes
become David's delight, affecting him like music, they were likewise
great treasure he discovered—honey, pleasant to his taste, and of more
value than silver and gold. May the Word of God excite the same wonder
in you as it did in David and give you a singing heart.

A Little Cloister within the Heart

"Thou wilt keep him in perfect peace, whose mind is
stayed on thee." *Isaiah 26:3.*

When Catherine of Siena was only a girl, she chafed against the family
claims and duties and longed for the solitude of a convent cell. A wise
teacher, however, bade her remember that she could always keep a little
cell within her own heart to which, in the midst of outward occupations,
she could inwardly retire and find a deeper peace for which she longed.
St. Theresa of Avila called it an "interior castle of the soul" that no
cares or fears could storm. As we know from Paul's teaching, at the
door of this innermost fortress God's peace stands as sentinel, challeng-
ing every thought that seems to enter and chasing away every harassing
form of anxiety. How blessed we are if we have discovered this secret
place of peace to which we can retreat in the most crowded hours of life.

In *The Spiritual Guide* the Spanish mystic Molinos said: "This Divine
Lord desires only that He may rest in thy soul, and may form therein
a rich throne of peace, that within thine own heart, by means of internal
recollection, and with His heavenly grace, thou mayest find silence in
tumult, solitude in company, light in darkness, forgetfulness in injuries,
vigor in despondency, courage in alarms, resistance in temptations, peace
in war, and quiet in tribulation."

Can we say that we walk with God amid the crowded duties of life
in such a way that we can sink deep into the quietness which is within
and not without, and then emerge, as it were, from that stillness at a
word, at a touch, and yet remain within it? Charles Wesley would have
us sing:

> *Here I find a house of prayer,*
> *To which I inwardly retire,*
> *Walking unconcerned in care,*
> *And unconsumed in fire.*

In the Heavens Write Your Glorious Name

"Upon the stone a new name written, which no one
knoweth but he that received it." *Revelation 2:17*, RV.

Edmund Spenser was a spiritual poet of the sixteenth century. In his
poem "Amoretti" he described how a name was traced in the sand, only
to be washed away by the waves, but that there was a name that would
never die in dust:

> *And in the heavens write your glorious name,*
> *Where when as death shall all the world subdue,*
> *Our love shall live, and later life renew.*

John assured us that God writes such an imperishable name upon a
white stone and gives it to every victorious child of his. What can this
promise mean but that the experience of God within each believer's heart
is individual, secret, and uncommunicable? Does this new and undis-
closed name by which God himself is made known to the soul suggest
that God discloses himself in some unique and personal way to each
faithful heart? Can it be that we find in God the completion of our own
distinctive lives, the answer to our own solitary needs, and a name that
stands for all that he is to *each of us*? Can it be that this new and secret
name is a particular name God chooses for, and bestows upon, the child
of God?

If this is the explanation, then we have the gracious suggestion of
the tenderness and intimacy of God's ways with his redeemed ones. For
each of us he has his own name that expresses what he alone sees. It is
comforting to know that we are to carry in our hearts like an amulet
the white stone with its new name written thereon, a token of all that
is between the glorified one and his God, a name no other knows, for
no one can tell to another all he or she has found in God.

HOLIDAYS
and
HARVESTS

Dry August and warm
Doth harvest no harm.

—Thomas Tusser,
"August's Husbandry"

A Commodity We Can All Buy

"Redeeming the time, because the days are evil."
Ephesians 5:16.

Modern translations of Paul's exhortation on "redeeming the time" are varied and profitable: "Making the most of your time" (RSV); "Making the most of every opportunity" (C. B. Williams); "Buying up every opportunity" (Amplified Bible). The latter interpretation is significant, for time is a commodity we can all buy and use to the best advantage. Said Benjamin Franklin, "Dost thou love life? Then do not squander *time,* for that is the stuff life is made of." Our employment of time shapes our character and determines our eternity. How rich in significance are the lines of Tennyson in "Lockley Hall":

Love took up the glass of Time, and turn'd it in his glowing hands;
Every moment, lightly shaken, ran itself in golden sands.

What wisdom we can gain from "the great Instructor, *Time.*" A plaque in my home bears this motto:

TIME IS
    Too slow for those who wait,
    Too swift for those who fear,
    Too long for those who grieve,
    Too short for those who rejoice,
    But for those who love
        TIME IS ETERNITY

People speak of "killing time." Let us not be guilty of such murder but realize that time comes each new day, hand in hand with its companion, opportunity. All who have time have opportunity—the privilege of serving God and humanity. If we lose time, opportunity slips away from us too. If we deliberately kill time, then opportunity lies dead at our feet. Because our days are so evil, may we be found buying up every opportunity to glorify God in our personal advance in holiness and in warning the lost to get right with God while they have time to seek him in penitence and faith. Only thus can we leave behind footprints on the sands of time for others to follow.

Who Like Thyself My Guide and Stay Shall Be?

"Thou shalt guide me with thy counsel." *Psalm 73:24.*

John Bunyan would have us remember that:

> *He that is ever humble,*
> *Has God to be his Guide.*

A guide, Webster informed us, is one who directs, regulates, orders, superintends the training of, instructs. He who has promised to be our guide, even unto death, functions in all these ways. And in the Book of Common Prayer we read, "Where Thou art Guide no ill can come."

Not only does God guide us unto death, but beyond it, for the psalmist affirmed that when guidance by divine counsel ends, "and afterward receive me to glory" (Ps. 73:24). But if we are to experience how the Lord can guide us continually, we must surrender entirely to him to be guided how and where he pleases. We must trust him implicitly to know all the future holds, and being infinitely gracious, perfectly wise, and immutably faithful, he is able to direct our steps aright. We must be careful about taking one step without his orders and aid.

It is blessed to know that all whom God guides he protects from foes, preserves amid trials, and provides in any time of need. Having redeemed us by the blood of his dear Son, God has made us his charge and care, and he will superintend all that concerns us until we reach the throne of his glory. His reputation as a perfect guide has never been tarnished. He never loses his way and has never lost a follower. Well might we sing with all faith and confidence these words by William Williams:

> *Guide me, O Thou great Jehovah,*
> *Pilgrim through this barren land.*

Like Children with Violets Playing

"Except ye turn, and become as little children, ye shall in no wise enter the kingdom of heaven." *Matthew 18:3*, RV.

A saint of a few centuries ago prayed that "each day and every day I surrender myself utterly and in all things to Divine Providence . . . like a little child in the bosom of its good and tenderhearted mother, to want everything and yet to want nothing—everything that God wills, nothing that He does not will." Mother Julian of Norwich spoke of God as "our courteous Mother." Like children who have fallen in the mud, we pray, "My kind Mother, I have made myself foul and unlike to Thee, and I neither may, nor can, amend it but with Thine help and grace." Jesus said we must exhibit this trustful life of a little child if we would enter heaven. St. Theresa of Lisieux called it the "Little Way," or the way of the little child. Jesus told Nicodemus that he must be born anew if he would see the kingdom of God.

Until we become as little children, weak and frail and having no strength of our own, we are not able to receive all "our courteous Mother" waits to give us. Many are too proud, self-willed, and self-sufficient to be saved. They scorn the helplessness of a little child. St. Augustine lamented, "Behold my childhood is dead!" But the childhood Jesus spoke of as being essential for the assurance of eternal life can be acquired anew into undying life.

In the face of a child there are no hard and haughty lines of self-pride, no blatant self-assertion. There is only the look of helplessness and dependence upon others. When the Spirit of God convicts a sinner of his or her need, the sinner in self-abhorrence and as a weak child, rests a feeble hand in the mighty hand of God and is at peace.

Fear Not, but Trust in Providence

"All things work together for good." *Romans 8:28.*

Before we consider all the glorious truths wrapped up in these six simple words, it must be emphasized that the providential goodness of God does not extend to all. No one can have the assurance that God is overruling in one's life, protecting, preserving, and providing for the person, *unless* one loves God and has been called according to one's purpose. Only the Christian can view *everything* as having a place in God's plan for his or her life.

All things. This means all circumstances, events, and experiences, whether pleasing or painful, are directed by God to fulfill his purpose and end. Omnipotence has servants everywhere, and whether they come dressed in gay colors or garments of distress and sorrow, the child of God is assured that God is able to bring good even out of evil.

Work. This word suggests planning and activity. Day by day God labors at his task of seeing that we never lose anything worth keeping of his dispensations.

Together. Harmony and unison are associated with his adverb. Because of God's perfect wisdom, there is never any conflict in his ordering of our lives. In his marvelous way he is able to fit all the pieces into a complete pattern. Those who love him know that nothing can occur which ought not to arise and that with him nothing is out of joint. Because of all he is in himself, God can make no mistakes. Thus the true believer in the spirit of true resignation can pray, "What Thou sendest is best."

Good. The harmonious overruling of our gains and losses, joys and sorrows, successes and failures, results in our present and eternal benefit. J. J. Lynch wrote:

> *Say not my soul, "From whence can God relieve my care?"*
> *Remember that Omnipotence has servants everywhere.*
> *His method is sublime, His heart profoundly kind,*
> *God never is before His time, and never is behind.*

Enslave Me with Thy Matchless Love

"Present your bodies a living sacrifice." Romans 12:1.

Paul, with his expert knowledge of the Jewish ritual of sacrifice, knew that when a beast was set apart for sacrifice it was considered sacred and was carefully preserved from all disease or injury. The apostle, spiritualizing the offering up of a lamb without blemish, said that the Christian is intended for the altar, not as a *dead* offering, but as a *living* sacrifice, holy and acceptable to God. Not only his body but all he represents must be kept from defilement, being daily cleansed by obedience to God's Word. Such a holy sacrifice is not only well-pleasing to God but is our "spiritual service of worship."

This presentation of ourselves is not the sullen submission of those who have been beaten but a joyful surrender or yielding up of ourselves to him who gave his all for us and therefore reserves our best. Certainly, we are to become his captives, but *willing* ones, ever ready to follow him in his triumph. Only when we are enslaved with his matchless love can we move freely.

The full surrender to God of all we are and have does not mean the loss of individuality. In the sacrifice of ourselves each of us finds a deeper, fuller life. Giving back the life each of us owes, we find that in God's deep love, life's flower becomes richer. Yielding ourselves as clay to the potter, we discover how he can mold us into a beauty we could not develop. As James Montgomery has taught us to sing:

> *Then with the gift of holiness within us;*
> *We not less human, but made more divine;*
> *Our lives replete with Heaven's supernal beauty,*
> *Ever declare that beauty, Lord, is Thine.*

Oh, To Be Content

"I have learned . . . to be content." *Philippians 4:11.*

Evidently Paul had reached the contented state, but when he used the word *content*, he did not mean what has been described as the torpor of a foul tranquility. What he implied was the acceptance of inevitable conditions as the sphere in which we are to do the will of God. "I know how to be abased, and I know how to abound," he reminded the Philippians (4:12). By divine grace Paul could handle both poverty and prosperity as they alternated in his experience because at all times he sought the kingdom of God and his righteousness.

Only as we seek the will of God in all circumstances can we possess an inward peace that enables us to find the most profitable way of dealing with every kind of situation. *Discontent* is written large over present-day society and causes so much of our industrial strife. Not content with such things as they have, people want more and still more. Solomon could write of one who would not "rest content, though thou givest many gifts" (Prov. 6:35). Our Lord told the soldiers of his day, "Be content with your wages" (Luke 3:14). Today the word is *contest*, not *content*. Unfortunately, some seem to have no regard whatever for the hardship they inflict upon others as they strike for what they want. But *godliness with contentment* is ever great gain, no matter what our material position may be.

Travel Stains of the Day

> "He who has bathed needs only to wash his feet . . . you
> are clean, but not all of you." *John 13:1–15*, RV.

Washing the disciples' feet in the Upper Room at the Last Supper was more than a sign of Jesus' love for his friends. It was even more than a lesson for them, and us, in the dignity of lowly service. In light of the conversation between Jesus and Peter, the feet-washing was an acted parable having a twofold application. First, Jesus was facing his betrayal, and he knew that Judas, whose heart had resisted him, would sell him to his enemies. But the rest of the disciples loved him. They were all clean, but Judas was not, and he died tragically in his uncleanness. "The Lord knoweth them that are his" (2 Tim. 2:19) and whose hearts have been "sprinkled from an evil conscience," whose bodies have been "washed with pure water" (Heb. 10:22). He made them clean, and they are his.

Second, every saint needs a daily cleansing from the travel stains of the road. Coming home from the dusty lanes, the traveler does not need to wash all over again; he needs only to wash his feet. The soul made clean by the blood cannot be reborn a second time; yet he does need a daily renewal of cleansing by which the travel stains are washed from his feet.

Ye are clean. What comfort there is in this truth! We learn from an unknown source:

> Once, definitely and irrevocably, we have been bathed in
> the crimson tide that flows from Calvary; but we need a
> daily cleansing. Our feet become soiled with the dust of
> life's highways; our hands grimy, as our linen beneath
> the rain of filth in a great city; our lips—as the white
> doorstep of the house—are fouled by the incessant throng
> of idle, unseemly, and fretful words; our hearts cannot
> keep unsoiled the stainless robes with which we pass
> from the closet at morning prime.

Before we retire at night, we need cleansing from the contagion of the world's slow stain.

The Morning Watch

"In the morning . . . Jesus rose up . . . and prayed."
Mark 1:35.

Many who love the Lord are able to give more extended hours than others to set seasons for prayer. But for the majority of saints who have to work, the day demands mental or physical exercise, with very little time for relaxation or spiritual worship. Hence it is necessary to begin each day with God in order to prepare for arduous tasks ahead and to receive poise and balance to live and labor through the working hours of the day as those who have a friend at hand. We read that this friend, whose days were crowded with preaching, teaching, and miracle works, rose "a great while before day . . . and departed into a desert place, and there prayed" (Mark 1:35, RV).

We may have no desert place to retire to in order to prepare ourselves prayerfully for the day ahead; yet we must each have a quiet spot within our homes where we can begin the day with God. If we are not able to provide spaces of silence and solitude in our daily life, times consecrated to the business of prayer, it is essential to maintain the morning watch with as much time as possible. If we start the day prayerless, we cannot expect to be kept in perfect peace as we meet problems, responsibilities, and decisions.

Mechthild of Magdeburg, a thirteenth-century German woman mystic, would have us remember:

> Prayer makes a sour heart sweet, a sad heart merry, a
> poor heart rich, a foolish heart wise, a timid heart
> courageous, a sick heart well, a blind heart full of vision,
> a cold heart ardent. For it draws down the great God
> into the little heart; it drives the hungry soul up to the
> plentitude of God; it brings together those two lovers,
> God and the soul.

Therefore, after we rise in the morning, let us meet the lover of our souls and with him journey through the rest of the day. "Early will I seek thee" (Ps. 63:1).

Far Beyond My Depth

"Hast thou entered into the springs of the sea? Or hast thou walked in the recesses of the deep?" *Job 38:16*, RV.

St. Teresa of Avila used to say that "it is only in this life that we have the chance of walking by faith and not by sight." When with our glorified beings we are with God, we will have the privilege of walking in the recesses of the deep truths of his being and character as we cannot presently do with our finite minds. Now he is past finding out, but in heaven what wonderful revelations of the mystery of his ways will be granted us.

As nature has her secrets, so has God, and until he reveals them unto us, we can but trust his wisdom and his love. We are indeed wise when we confess that human knowledge, no matter how extensive it may be, has its bounds beyond which it cannot pass. With all our searching, we cannot find God out. We are no more able to fathom deep and dark truths, or to discover the reason of his providences, the motive of his actions, the design of his visitation, that we can comprehend the depth from which the ancient ocean draws her watery stores. Charles H. Spurgeon, nineteenth-century English preacher, wrote:

Let me not strive to understand the infinite, but spend
my strength in love. What I cannot gain by intellect I can
possess by affection, and let that suffice me. I cannot
penetrate the heart of the sea, but I can enjoy the healthful
breezes which sweep over its bosom, and I can sail over
its blue waves with propitious winds.

Love to God and obedience to his will are more profitable than trying to walk in the recesses of the deep. Thus we pray, My Lord, I leave the infinite to Thee, and pray Thee to put far from me such a love for the tree of knowledge as might keep me from the tree of life!

The Crown of Love and Friendship

"Abraham my friend." *Isaiah 41:8.*

How rich in suggestion is John Keats's tribute to divine friendship in his poem "Endymion":

> *Wherein lies happiness? In that which beckons*
> *Our ready minds to fellowship divine,*
> *A fellowship with essence.*
> > *The crown of these*
> *Is made of love and friendship, and sits high*
> *Upon the forehead of humanity.*

Abraham, more than any other person, seems to have had such "fellowship with essence" in abundance, for God called him *my friend.* Jehoshaphat spoke to God of "Abraham thy friend for ever" (2 Chron. 20:7); while James says of the patriarch, "He was called the Friend of God" (Jas. 2:23). Although so highly privileged, Abraham was not alone in wearing upon his forehead the crown of divine friendship. Cowper wrote:

> *Throned above the heights He condescends,*
> *To call the few that trust in Him, His friends.*

Jesus said to his disciples, "No longer do I call you servants . . . but friends" (John 15:15, RV). Through grace we too are brought into a fellowship of heart and mind, a sharing of the thoughts and purposes of Jesus. How arrestive are Shakespeare's lines in *Hamlet*:

> *Those friends thou hast, and their adoption tried,*
> *Grapple them unto thy soul with hoops of steel.*

As Jesus is the friend who sticks closer to us than a brother, may we be found grappling him to our hearts with hoops of steel. He laid down his life for his friends—and enemies.

Every Creature . . . Depends on His Creator

"Apart from Me you can do nothing." *John 15:5*, ASB.

Nature is a parable of God, and in each of her forms we have a revelation of God. In using the emblem of the vine and its branches, Jesus illustrated and enforced the truth of our utter dependence upon him. Both the vine and its branches constitute one plant, and Jesus and his own are one. The vine root is not sufficient in itself; it must have branches to bear the fruit. It is the same with him who called himself the true vine; he has fruit-bearing branches, or "long lines of saved souls extending down the centuries—through which to communicate Himself to a barren world." So wrote Alexander Smellie, renowned early twentieth-century Scottish minister.

The fruit comes from the sap in the main stem. Thus, Smellie said, "the vine is in the branch; no self-sustained life is throbbing through twigs and tendrils; they are dependent for all that they are and all that they can produce on the quickening currents, that flow to them from the root and stem of the tree."

From me is thy fruit found. As all the life of the vine lives in each fragile tendril and as all the fruitfulness of the vine finds its fulfillment in each branch containing all the sweetness of the vine in each cluster, so all the life and grace and beauty of Jesus dwells in you and me as branches. Since branches can only live and bear fruit as they abide in the vine, apart from him we are but fruitless, withering branches.

Andrew Murray, South African leader of the Dutch Reformed Church who died in 1917, exhorted us:

> Think not so much of thyself as a Branch, nor of the
> abiding as thy duty, until thou hast first had thy soul
> filled with the faith of what Christ as the Vine is. He
> will really be to thee all that a vine can be, holding thee
> fast, nourishing thee, and making Himself every moment
> responsible for thy growth and fruit.

He is indeed the true life-giving vine.

Patient Endurance Is Godlike

"After he had patiently endured he obtained the promise." Hebrews 6:15.

Longfellow gave us this impressive phrase from "Evangeline": "Sorrow and silence are strong, and patient endurance is godlike." Abraham had plenty of "sorrow and silence," and they helped to make him the strong character he became. By his godlike patient endurance he inherited and obtained the promises of God (Heb. 6:12, 15).

The word used here for *patience* means more than endurance. It is the word elsewhere rendered *long-suffering*. It is active rather than passive. There was "faith in patience," and the safe cure for sluggishness is ever the activity which persists in conforming the life and its habits to the faith which is professed, even as Abraham did.

Long and sorely tried, this friend of God never questioned God's delay in fulfilling his promise. There is no evidence of his doubting God's veracity, limiting his power, questioning his faithfulness, or grieving his love. Ultimately, Abraham received the promise of a son because he bowed to divine sovereignty, submitted to divine wisdom, and was silent under delays, waiting God's time. As a patient waiter Abraham has left us an example to imitate. His manner of life wrote an unknown author, "condemns a hasty spirit, reproves a murmuring one, commends a patient one, and encourages quiet submission to God's will and way." We sing with Thomas Olivers:

> *The God of Abraham praise,*
> *Whose all-sufficient grace*
> *Shall guide me all my happy days*
> *In all my ways.*
> *He calls a worm His friend: He calls Himself my God:*
> *And He shall save me to the end, Through Jesus' blood.*

Freedom Has a Thousand Charms to Show

"The truth shall make you free." *John 8:32.*

In "Table Talk" Cowper informs us that:

> *Freedom has a thousand charms to show,*
> *That slaves, howe'er contented, never know.*

The emancipating truth Jesus taught has indeed a "thousand charms" and proclaims a glorious liberty of which contented slaves of sin are grossly ignorant. There is the *double curse*, for sin both *blinds* and *binds*. That it blinds is evident from the assertion of the Jews who listened to what Jesus had to say about freedom and said, "We were never in bondage to any man." Somehow they had forgotten the long and bitter slavery of Egypt. Prejudice had blinded them. "The eyes of their understanding are darkened" (Eph. 4:18, paraphrase).

Sin binds and enslaves those who began by thinking they could take up sin and lay it down at their will. They became slaves of sin. But, through grace, there is *the double cure*, for, as the hymnist John Addington Symonds, put it, there is a "loftier race":

> *With flame of freedom in the souls,*
> *And light of knowledge in their eyes.*

Our Lord's two phrases the "Son shall make you free" and "The truth shall make you free" are not contradictory but complementary, for he said, "I am . . . the truth" (John 14:6). Freedom from the tyranny of sin must come from without, and it has through him who by his mastery over Satan and sin provided a glorious liberty for all who receive him.

But spiritual freedom does not mean that we may do as we like. Deliverance from sin does not imply license. In the Lord's service there is perfect freedom to do only what pleases our blessed emancipator.

It Becometh Well the Just to be Thankful

"In everything give thanks." *1 Thessalonians 5:18.*

Each of us should pray daily the following petition which is found in the Anglican Order of Service: "We beseech Thee to make us truly sensible of Thy mercy, and give us hearts always ready to express our thankfulness, not only by words, but also by our lives, in being more obedient to Thy holy commandments."

In Paul's quartet of words there are precious truths to ponder. *In.* The apostle did not say *"for* everything give thanks," and we are glad. Certain calamities overtake us for which . . . we cannot kneel down and express gratitude. But we can give thanks *in* them because we know that our all-wise God never makes a mistake and that what he permits must be for his glory and our good.

Everything. Paul did not say *some* things but *everything.* We find it easy to be grateful for the good things of life but not for the bitter cup. Yet the dark threads are as needful as the threads of gold and silver in God's pattern for your life and mine. Apart from his supporting grace it is hard to pray as did an unknown writer:

> *Through dark and dearth, through fire and frost,*
> *With emptied arms and treasures lost,*
> *I thank Thee while my days go on.*

Give. This is a sacrificial word and implies, as Whittier suggested, "each loving life a psalm of gratitude." Are we not enjoined to "offer the *sacrifice of praise* continually" (Heb. 13:15)? We must take time to meditate upon all the benefits so freely and fully bestowed and praise him from whom all blessings flow.

Thanks. Thanksgiving for all things is never out of season, for we have always so much to be thankful for, and gratitude pleases the bountiful giver. With another unknown writer we sing:

> *A thousand blessings, Lord, to us Thou dost impart,*
> *We ask one blessing more, O Lord,—a thankful heart!*

A Double Bounty

"The Lord will give grace and glory." *Psalm 84:11.*

The gifts of God are as freely given to man as the light of the sun, and two of these gifts are grace and glory. Spurgeon wrote that "the little conjunction *and* in this verse is a diamond rivet binding the present with the future: grace and glory always go together. God has married them, and none can divorce them. The Lord will never deny a soul *glory* to whom He has freely given to live upon His grace." *Grace.* If you drop the *G*, you have *race*, and Grace has been abundantly given for all within the human race, for God so loved the world. All who repent and believe can receive the free gift of grace. Then when we are saved by grace, he gives us more grace. No matter how good a person may try to be, no merit can entitle a sinner to grace, which God gives liberally to the repentant, believing sinner. To all who are redeemed, grace in all its forms he freely renders. Grace is to fit us for service, support us in trial, and sanctify our hearts. All we are and have is of his matchless grace.

Glory. What is glory but grace in perfection? If by his grace we have been saved, then we shall be glorified with him. He cannot deny glory to those to whom he has given grace. To quote Spurgeon again, "Glory is nothing more than grace in its Sabbath dress, grace is full bloom, grace like autumn fruit, mellow and perfected. Glory, the glory of Heaven, to glory of Eternity, the glory of Jesus, the glory of the Father, the Lord will surely give to His chosen". So let us cling to this rare promise of our faithful God. Two lines by an unknown writer are inspiring:

> *Two golden links of one celestial chain:*
> *Who owneth grace shall surely glory gain.*

A Sabbath of the Heart

"A rest for the people of God . . . . Give diligence to enter that rest." *Hebrews 4:9, 11.*

That the Bible is a manual on the necessity and methods of rest is proven by the fact that the word *rest*, as applied to spiritual relaxation, occurs over two hundred times. Rest is a gift of heaven, yet something we must find. Peace, concord, silence, quietness, to be at ease, and to lean or rely upon are some of the various meanings of our English word *rest*. In several passages it means Sabbath. Thus Dryden wrote about breaking "the eternal Sabbath of his rest." Wordsworth used the same thought:

> . . . Every day should leave some part
> Free for a Sabbath of the heart;
> So shall the Seventh be truly blest,
> From morn to eve with hallowed rest.

The rest that remains is not in heaven alone; it is for all the people of God on earth to enter into deeply and possess as they linger amid the shadows. Such a rest does not imply cessation from work or freedom from conflict and suffering. God's ideal for us is "in our labour rest most sweet." Cowper expresses it:

> Absence of occupation is not rest,
> A mind quite vacant is a mind distress'd.

The true rest we are to seek diligently comes when we cease from self and find our all in Jesus. In his rest he gathers round our restlessness, as Robert Browning puts it. This rest is not so much a possession as a person. "*Thou* art my Rest." The Lord is the true peace of the heart; out of him there is nothing but disquiet and restlessness. What a Sabbath for the heart it is to rest *in* him with unshaken, confiding, and ardent love.

They Came at a Delicate Plain Called Ease

". . . His soul shall dwell at ease." Psalm 25:13.

While the noun *ease* is understood as meaning freedom from pain, annoyance, constraint, effort, or anything that disquiets or oppresses, in the verse before us the term does not imply laziness or indolence. A "woe" was pronounced upon those who were at ease in Zion. God never intended any child of his to live idly. "Son, go work today in my vineyard" (Matt. 21:28). Shakespeare could have the ghost find Hamlet "duller . . . than the fat weed that rots itself in ease." In the original Hebrew text, *ease* has several meanings. In the verse above it means "good," and so the phrase has been translated, "His soul shall lodge in goodness" or "His soul will abide in prosperity." In the darkest, saddest, loneliest hour, the soul can find a home in the goodness of God. Our hearts can be free from slavish fears and from soul-distressing anxieties and dwell in a state of contentment and solid peace only when we place our faith in God's Word. Our cares are replaced with a realization of his omniscience and omnipresence, a longing to please him in all things, a fear to offend him in anything, and an unceasing desire for his return.

Beloved, has your soul found a resting place in which your heart is at ease because you are at peace with God? Are you lodging in the goodness of God who is the storehouse of every blessing, the supply of every need, and the one who alone can silence all our fears? Undue and unbelieving anxiety about anything vanishes as we cast all our cares upon God and live on "the delicate plain, called *Ease*," as John Bunyan expressed it. With God as our portion, his precious promises are as security, his glorious atonement as our plea, Jesus as our constant advocate, and heaven as our final home, why should we charge our soul with any care? May grace be ours to be at home in ease.

God's Nonconformists

"Be not conformed to this world." *Romans 12:2.*

Emerson said that "whoso would be a man must be a non-conformist." In modern parlance, a nonconformist does not adhere to the order of the established Church of England; a conformist acts in harmony with all the edicts of the church. All who are members of the church, which is the body of Christ, are nonconformists since they do not agree with the ways of a godless world. Every believer should have a nonconformist conscience when it comes to separation from the world. Are we not urged to come out from among unbelievers and touch not the unclean thing? If we confess to be Christians, let us be marked and distinct Christians.

The miracle of Pentecost was the placing of the church in the world. The masterpiece of Satan is placing of the world in the church, which results in spiritual barrenness. The church's Pentecostal power has been lost through its conformity to the world. Spurgeon said:

> Would you attain the full assurance of faith? you cannot
> gain it while you commune with sinners. Would you
> flame with vehement love? your love will be damped by
> the drenchings of godless society. You cannot become a
> great Christian—you may be a babe in grace, but you
> never can be a perfect man in Christ Jesus while you yield
> yourself to worldly maxims and modes of business of men
> of the world. It is ill for an heir of Heaven to be a great
> friend with heirs of Hell.

That Jesus was an unflinching, unashamed nonconformist can be gathered from his explicit declaration, "I am not of the world." And he spoke of his own as being in harmony with his nonconformity, "Ye are not of this world" (John 17:16).

The First-rate for the Having

"But seek ye first the kingdom of God and his righteousness." *Matthew 6:33.*

One of the most colorful and controversial figures in English life and literature is Malcolm Muggeridge. In the second volume of his entertaining autobiography *The Infernal Grove* he is by turn elegant, amusing, and sour, but always honest about himself, as the following quotation proves: "The saddest . . . thing to me . . . is the preference I have so often shown for what is inferior, tenth-rate, when the first-rate was there for the having."

Is this not the folly of many who seek the fleshpots of Egypt rather than the kingdom of God and his righteousness? They prefer the tenth-rate of the Devil rather than the first-rate Jesus urges us to seek. But why hanker after the inferior when the superior is for the having? A place in God's kingdom and being robed in his righteousness are ever first-rate even though all else of inferior value be ours.

The caesars of Rome had all they could wish for in wealth, palaces, slaves, and soldiers. Were they happy and content with such inferior possessions? No. From an unknown source we learn that "Augustus became morose and suspicious in his old age; Tiberius fled from Rome to the loneliness and sin of the little island of Capri; Nero had to hide at last from his enemies in a miserable hut outside the city." Because God made us for himself, we must seek him first and always. Georgiana M. Taylor wrote:

Seek ye first, not earthly pleasure,
Fading joy and failing treasure,
But the Love that knows no measure
Seek ye first.

May None Those Marks Efface!

"The print of the nails." *John 20:25.*

Byron in his "Sonnet on Chillon" wrote the following lines:

> . . . *May none those marks efface!*
> *For they appeal from tyranny to God.*

The marks Jesus eternally bears appeal from the tyranny of those who caused God in the dateless past to surrender his beloved son to be a sacrifice for the sins of the world. None will ever be able to efface the marks of the nails in his hands and feet, for they represent our eternal salvation. They are marks of indelible grace, and eternity cannot erase them. We shall know our Redeemer by the print of the nails in his hands, when redeemed by his side we stand. Cruel men pierced his hands and feet, but the only cry the pain wrung from his lips was a prayer for his enemies. The blood from his gaping wounds became the blood of redemption. Charles Wesley sang:

> *Five bleeding wounds He bears, received on Calvary;*
> *They pour effectual prayers, they strong plead for me.*
> *"Forgive him, oh, forgive," they cry,*
> *"Let not that ransomed sinner die."*

Staupitz cried to Martin Luther, "Look at the wounds of Jesus!" and there is no other way by which a sinner can be saved. Thomas said he would not believe what others said about Jesus unless he saw the print of the nails, and when Jesus showed him his hands and his side, Thomas cried, "My Lord and my God!" (John 20:28). Any religion or plan of salvation destitute of the print of the nails is to be rejected. Paul prayed that he might bear in his body the Calvary marks of the Lord Jesus. Crucified hands are careful what they handle; crucified feet are careful where they go; crucified hearts are careful who and what they love.

He Views His Children with Delight

"The Lord takes pleasure in them that fear him, in those that hope in his mercy." *Psalm 147:11.*

Mother Julian of Norwich loved to write of the saints as "the bliss of the Lord." In *Revelation of Divine Love* she said:

Our good Lord said blissfully, Lo, *I have loved thee*, as if He had said, . . . See what satisfying and bliss I have in thy salvation, and rejoice with Me. . . . Now in all My bitter pain and all My hard travail turned to endless joy and bliss to Me and to thee.

Thomas Traherne in the seventeenth century expressed the same thought of divine delight in his poem:

> *. . . O my soul, ours is far most bliss*
> *Than His is ours; at least it so doth seem*
> *Both in His own and our esteem.*

Jesus finds a deep and satisfying joy in those who have been redeemed by his blood and are lovingly obedient to his will. God could say of him, "This is my beloved Son, in whom I am well pleased" (Matt. 3:17). As the sons of God through grace, ours is the privilege of giving God pleasure. It is on record that Job was well-pleasing unto God. Then it seems as if God almost boasted about Job when he asked, "Hast thou considered my servant Job? For there is none like him in the earth" (Job 1:8).

Does he find the same pleasure or bliss in you and me? Is he delighted in us since we love him, share his thoughts, and serve the cause so dear to his own heart? Is he not saddened when he cannot find in us the fellowship he desires? May we so live in unison with his will that he will rejoice over us with singing. Truly, we are his bliss, as we know from the following lines by an unknown author:

> *But saints are lovely in His sight,*
> *He views His children with delight;*
> *He sees their hope, He knows their fear,*
> *And looks, and loves His image there.*

My Life Is by His Counsel Planned

"My times are in thy hand." Psalm 31:15.

What a consoling affirmation this is! When we remember that the ordering of our lives rests in God's hand, what peace of mind should be ours. His omnipotent hand also controls the universe and the destinies of nations. Job reminded us that "times are not hidden from the Almighty" (Job 24:1). This truth prevents us from looking at God through circumstances; instead we should look at circumstances through the environing presence of him whose powerful hand none can stay. God measures out our days, and our hours should obey his loving will.

It is not by chance that we are living in these times, for his will chose this day in which we live, and we must not drift unseeing through such a time of divine opportunity. These are indeed hard and difficult times, but all events are under divine control, nothing being left to chance. Does it not comfort your heart to know that the hand of God is in all that occurs, directing and overruling and sanctifying for our present and eternal good? Whether our times are glad or sad, God knows best about the daily ordering of the course of our lives. William F. Floyd wrote:

> *My times are in Thy hand, Whatever they may be;*
> *Pleasing or painful, dark or bright, As best may seem to Thee.*

The psalmist told us that by being in God's hand he is able to deliver us from the hand of our enemies and persecutors. May grace be ours to rest in the assurance that, hour by hour, the varied experiences of life are shaped by God into his program for our lives. Floyd also wrote:

> *My times are in Thy hand; Why should I doubt or fear?*
> *My Father's hand will never cause His child a needless tear.*

See All, nor Be Afraid

"He shall not be afraid of evil tidings." *Psalm 112:7.*

The only thing a Christian has to fear is *fear* itself, and if our hearts are fixed by trust in the Lord, then of whom or what should we be afraid? Certainly there is much to be afraid of in the evil tidings our daily papers record of violence, hooliganism, crime, brutal murders, lack of integrity among men in high places, immorality, and war. No wonder people are scared as they think of the future; their hearts fail them for fear. But deliverance from all fear possesses the hearts of those who believe that there is no cold fate, no blind, unpredictable chance controlling the world, but a heavenly, loving Father. Clouds may gather, but they will pass away or break in showers of mercy.

A cynic said to a Christian friend, "If I could see all God sees of evil and tragedy in the world, it would break my heart!"

The friend quietly replied, "But God's heart did break at Calvary for the sin of the world."

The godless have every reason to be afraid of evil tidings because they have no God to fly to, no *hid security*, as Rupert Brooke expressed it. If those of us who are the Lord's are distracted and distraught by the state of the world, then where is the value of that grace we profess to have received from him who would have us live without fear? If we gave way to alarm in the day of evil tidings, unable to meet trouble with that calm composure, nerving us for service and sustaining us under adversity, how can we expect to honor him who said, "Let not your heart be troubled, neither let it be afraid" (John 14:27)? Because the days are evil, we must be holy and thereby act as the salt of the earth, arresting its corruption. Let us be found combatting evil tidings by proclaiming the good tidings of the Gospel.

The Fear That Sends Me to His Breast

"Fear him . . . yea, I say unto you, fear him." *Luke 12:4–5.*

Although as Christians we meet evil tidings with the absence of fear, but there is a fear we must earnestly cultivate, and it is the fear of the Lord. Scripture has a great deal to say about this kind of fear. Jesus told his friends not to be afraid even of those who would seek to kill them, but he warned them to fear God who has power to cast evil men into hell. When this nobler fear dwells in the heart, there is no room for lesser fears. We cease to be afraid of what others can do against us, or of any stroke of trouble that may fall upon us, for such cannot touch one's real life—the hidden life of fellowship with God.

Fear, in respect to the Lord, is not the cringing fear of slaves for the cruel and callous master. Throughout the Old Testament the phrase "the fear of the Lord" represents piety and reverential trust coupled with hatred of evil. As David expressed it, "The fear of the Lord is clean, enduring for ever" (Ps. 19:9). This is the meaning Charles Wesley enshrined in his hymn:

> *Give me, Lord, a holy fear,*
> *And fix it in my heart,*
> *That I may from evil near*
> *With timely care depart;*
> *Sin be more than hell abhorred;*
> *Till Thou destroy the tyrant foe,*
> *Keep me, keep me, gracious Lord,*
> *And never let me go!*

May the Lord teach us to fear nothing but the sin that robs us of our holy fear of his name.

71

Man Is Immortal till His Work Is Done

"I must go on my way today and tomorrow and the day following." *Luke 13:33* (RSV).

The title of this meditation is of early origin, but in the seventeenth century Thomas Fuller in his *Church History of Britain* quoted an extended version of the saying: "God's children are immortal while their Father has anything for them to do on earth." Our Lord's specific pronouncement formed part of his answer to the Pharisees and to Herod, all of whom sought to kill him before his God-appointed time. He was immune from death, however, until the work he was sent to do was accomplished. Anticipating Calvary, he prayed to his Father, "I have finished the work thou gavest me to do" (John 17:4). The time periods *today* and *tomorrow* were the days when he would continue unhindered the exercise of his gracious ministry. The *day following* or the "third day" was to be the day he would be perfected, the day of his death, not by those of this earth, but by the prearranged counsel of God.

Whether our days are long or short makes little difference, for in the purpose of God it is not the length of life that counts but the quality of it. Jesus was some thirty-three years old when his task was finished, but what marvelous things he accomplished in those brief years. As we live in true fellowship with him, we have the assurance that until our life's work is ended no hostile power is strong enough to prevent us from finishing our course.

Matthew Henry commented, "It is a comfort to us, in reference to the power and malice of our enemies, that they can have no power to take us off as long as God has any work for us to do." We may lament when a child of God is suddenly cut off because unfinished tasks are left behind. But from the divine side, that person's task was completed— *it is finished.*

A Friend in Need Is a Friend Indeed

"Call upon me! . . . I will deliver." Psalm 50:15.

There is no uncertainty whatever about this divine promise. The Lord knows all about our troubles; so there is no need to give him information about them. But if we need his help, he demands that we should call. Days of troubles are often permitted to make us call, and when we are in need, the Lord is a friend indeed. Robert Browning said, "What if this friend happens to be—God?" The friend inviting us to let him know when we require his aid *is* God. The Apocrypha says that "A faithful friend is the medicine of life." How true this is of him who condescends to offer himself as our friend, who is always within call and has boundless resources to help us! He assures us that his ear is not so heavy that he cannot hear us, nor his arm shortened that it cannot help us.

When sore trials overtake us, we must not look to others to undertake for us until God has proved that he cannot or will not lift our burden—*and that will never be*! Because of all he is in himself and all that he has promised, he must respond as we arise and call upon him. God's heart is too kind and his word too faithful for him to turn a deaf ear to our entreaty.

Are you facing a *special* trouble? Without hesitation, pay God a visit, lay your whole case before him, and expect his sympathy, aid, and blessing. He will deliver you, and you shall glorify him. As you trust him as your friend, you honor him. As you expect him to undertake for you in the hour of your need, you have the assurance that you will not be ashamed, for he is ever to be found by those who seek him in all sincerity. *Ask, and ye shall receive.*

The King's Name Is a Tower of Strength

> "The name of the Lord is a strong tower: the righteous runneth into it, and is safe." *Proverbs 18:10.*

Shakespeare's praise of King Richard III is true of our heavenly King, whose varied names and titles reveal him to be *the* tower of strength to his people. In his "Ode on the Death of the Duke of Wellington" Tennyson wrote of the famous soldier:

> *O fall'n at length that tower of strength*
> *Which stood four-square to all the winds that blew.*

Since the fall of Lucifer, God has stood foursquare against all satanic blasts and assaults. He has not fallen and cannot since he is the eternal, impregnable tower of strength. What truth this promise holds for our hearts.

The name of the Lord. By his dear name, which is the rock on which I build, my shield and hiding place, we understand all that he is in himself. "As His name, so is He" (1 Sam. 25:25). His name, "sweet in a believer's ear," as a hymn states, represents his nature, character, and being.

Is a strong tower. The idea of the Lord as our refuge, hiding place, fortress, tower, and stronghold permeates Scripture. The strongest towers of men have fallen to enemies, but although the world around us is rocking to its foundations, God is a refuge that cannot be moved. When tumult rages, we have in him a strong citadel of calm.

The righteousness runneth into it. The provision of God as a tower is only for those who are clothed with his righteousness. For the godless there is no hiding place from wrath.

And is safe. Shelter and security are experienced by all those who find in his name a love that never fails, a sympathy always perfect, a sweet omnipotence of grace, and provision equal to every need.

Faint Not nor Fear, His Arms Are Near

"Underneath are the everlasting arms."
Deuteronomy 33:27.

Many figures of speech, like the one before us, have a touch of tender intimacy about them. It is no mere vague goodwill to which we commit ourselves, a kind of friendly tendency in the universe; we commit ourselves to one who personally cares and loves his children. As it is natural for children to run to the arms of their parents when little troubles overtake them, so it is natural for those who believe in the fatherhood of God to cast themselves into the arms of their heavenly Father when the trials of life beset them. J. Drummond Burns taught us to sing:

> *As helpless as a child who clings*
> *Fast to its father's arm,*
> *And casts his weakness on the strength*
> *That keeps him safe from harm:*
> *So I, my Father, cling to Thee,*
> *And thus I every hour*
> *Would link my earthly feebleness*
> *To Thine almighty power.*

The arms around and underneath us are the everlasting arms of the eternal God and are, therefore, well able to support and protect us at all times. Think of the double consolation there is for our hearts in the glorious promise, "The eternal God is thy dwelling-place." Our native environment is not earth or time but heaven and eternity. We are assured that the everlasting arms of our eternal God are underneath us, ever there to save us from falling. No matter how deep our distress and affliction may be, underneath are the arms that never flag or lose their strength, embracing and consoling us. Thus sustained, all Satan's efforts to harm us avail nothing. Fanny J. Crosby wrote:

> *Safe in the arms of Jesus,*
> *Safe on His gentle breast,*
> *There by His love o'ershaded,*
> *Sweetly my soul shall rest.*

The Garment of Praise for the Spirit of Heaviness

"My soul melteth for heaviness: strengthen thou me
according to thy word." *Psalm 119:28.*

Although the word *depression* is not in the Bible, all that it depicts is
scattered throughout the sacred pages and emerges in phrases like "Out
of the depths I cried unto Thee" (Ps. 130:1), "Why are thou cast down,
O my soul?" (Ps. 42:5), "When my spirit was overwhelmed within
me" (Ps. 142:3). David was often despondent. John Trapp, a seventeenth-century English Bible commentator, said of the psalmist's sigh,
"Why art thou cast down, O my soul," that "David chideth David out
of the dumps." His redeemed spirit rebukes the flesh and battles with
its despondency in the name of the most high.

All of us have days when a weight seems to lie on the spirit and the
soul melts for heaviness. A mist hangs over our world, work becomes
a weariness, and depression seizes us. Physical weakness or mental over-
strain produces moments of spiritual darkness and the drying up of
spiritual joy. When such heaviness of spirit overtakes us, a cure for our
depressed state of mind is to don the garment of praise—*Hope thou in
God*!

Brighter days dawn as we leave our brooding over troubles and go
out to help others who are downcast. John Keble's wise word is apt:
"When you find yourself overpowered as it were by melancholy, the
best way is to go out and do something kind to somebody or other."
New hope and strength are ours when we seek to carry cheerfully
another's load. The consoling thought is that even in the gloom Jesus
is with us. He promised to undertake for us "all the days"—days of
despondency and cheerless gloom as well as days of joyous sunshine.
"When my spirit was overwhelmed within me, thou knewest my path."
Only such a faith can save us from despair and bring to us treasures,
even out of our darkness.

The Superfluous Is Necessary

"How much more shall your Father which is in heaven
give good things?" *Matthew 7:11.*

The dictionary informs us that *superfluous* means "overflowing," "more than is necessary," "an excess of which is sufficient." As a professed atheist Voltaire did not have the superfluity of God in mind when he coined the phrase, "The superfluous is necessary." The *much more* that Jesus spoke reveals that our heavenly Father is not prescribed in his provision but superabundant. When Jesus fed the hungry crowds, there was not just enough to go around, but after all had eaten well, there was the superfluity of twelve baskets full of fragments. Such superfluity was necessary to prove that he is able to do exceeding abundantly, above all we ask for or need.

In his teaching Jesus interprets the bountiful heart of God. If an earthly father gives his child what he asks for—a loaf, stone, fish, or serpent—our heavenly Father waits to give his children greater and more numerous good things. So let us cling to these three words, *How much more!* Human love is a symbol of the divine, but the symbol often fails. "If ye then know how to give good gifts" (Matt. 7:11)—but fathers do not always know and in ignorance bestow gifts that prove detrimental. Our heavenly Father always knows what is best for every child of his and in his wise love gives only *good gifts*—his beloved Son, the Holy Spirit, the Holy Scriptures, his grace and glory. In God's giving we have a sea without a shore. Overflowing blessings are ours here and now, but the hand that bled to make them ours holds *much more* for us in heaven. Then we shall turn, as an unidentified author wrote,

> *From the gift looking to the Giver,*
> *And from the cistern to the River,*
> *And from the finite to Infinity,*
> *And from man's dust to God's divinity.*

More Space in My Narrow Heart

"Abraham called the name of that place Jehovah-jireh
[meaning the Lord will provide]." *Genesis 22:14.*

Frederick W. Faber told us in his hymn "Thou Broadenest Out with Every Year" that God makes more space for himself when he gives us a clearer vision of his face. After Abraham had witnessed what God did on the mount, he received, not only a further revelation of the Almighty, but more space in his heart for his friend.

Divine names and titles are a fascinating theme, as I have sought to show in my book on this subject. *Jehovah-jireh*, for instance, was not only a new name for a place, it was also a new name for God—a name registering a fuller discovery of God and an addition to Abraham's thought and experience of God. From now on the patriarch was to know him as *the Lord will provide*, the God intervening at the moment of need.

As we follow the list of names given to God, we find that each fresh one further revealed his love and power through some great experience. *Jehovah-nissi*, meaning the "Lord my banner," was another name born of a new sense of God's leadership and protection. Richard Baxter, seventeenth-century Puritan divine, could write, "Every state and change of my life, notwithstanding my sin, hath opened to me Treasures and Mysteries of Love, and after such a life of Love shall I doubt whether the same God do love me?"

Have we not had experiences, enriching our spiritual store with new thoughts of God and, like Abraham, found ourselves going forward with great assurance that he would provide? Coming to a mount of trial, we found it turned into a mount of mercy. "On the mount of the Lord he will be seen" (Gen. 22:14, R.V. margin). Only on the mounts of sorrows and testings do we come to know him as the one ready to supply our need and display his power on our behalf.

BEAUTY
and
BOUNTY

Up from the meadows rich with
corn
Clear is the cool September morn.

—John Greenleaf Whittier,
"Barbara Frietchie"

Thou Dost Preserve the Stars from Wrong

"O thou preserver of men." Job 7:20.

God not only preserves the stars from wrong and makes the ancient heavens fresh and strong, as Wordsworth expressed it, he also preserves the saints. Job had deep experiences of God's preserving grace and mercy, for he could say, "I have seen God face to face, and my life is preserved" (Gen. 32:30). We also have the assurance that God will preserve our going out and our coming in until traveling days are done. A modern translation (RSV) gives us, "O watcher of men," and the eye that is on the sparrow watches over us to preserve us from falling. Because of our inherent sinful nature we are liable to fall; we have neither the wisdom nor the strength to preserve ourselves from the hand of the enemy. Corruption within and without is strong, and our hearts are deceitful. Satan is ever vigilant to beguile us.

Therefore, we need a *preserver* every hour to call upon as we are assailed by the enemy, and God is such a one who can and does preserve his own. But divine preservation is ours only as we walk in the way of obedience. How can we expect his security if we are not watchful, prayerful, and walking humbly before him? Without his strong hand to keep us, we fall into the grossest sins. May we be delivered from the folly of thinking we are safe, except as we are found constantly leaning on him and daily cultivating communion with him who is able to keep us safe and secure. The world, the flesh, and the Devil are leagued against us, and nothing but omnipotent grace can preserve us from falling and ultimately present us faultless before the presence of his glory with exceeding joy. "I have heard thee . . . I will preserve thee" (Isa. 49:8).

The Liberality of Our Glorious Boaz

"And Ruth did eat, and was sufficed, and left." Ruth 2:14.

Within the world's literature, sacred and secular, no love story is so absorbing as that of Ruth the Moabitess who became the ancestress of the Lord Jesus Christ. Finding herself in Bethlehem, Ruth faced the practical problem of poverty. Looking for work, "her hap was to light on the portion of the field belonging unto Boaz" (2:3). The word *hap* does not mean that the meeting with Boaz was accidental but implies *that which she met with*—an issue revealing divine overruling. There are no accidents in the life of faith. In its music, the accidentals perfect the harmony.

During a break in the hard toil, Boaz was attracted by the charming maiden who had come to glean and offered Ruth some of his own parched corn. We read that "she did eat, and was sufficed and left" (2:14). Thomas Gray, poet of the seventeenth century, wrote of one, "Large was his bounty and his soul sincere." Such was certainly true of Boaz and truer of our heavenly Boaz whose liberality we magnify.

As Ruth was satisfied with the meal Boaz provided, what can we say about the bountiful repast our Lord provides? Where he is host, no guest goes empty from the table but is sufficed. All desires are satiated when we know him and are found in him. Sufficed, Ruth left. Is this not so with us? We have had deep drafts; we thought that we could take in all of Christ, but when we have done our best, we have had to leave a vast remainder. After leaving the satisfying meal, Ruth discovered that a richer bounty was to follow. Likewise we learn that after having our hunger relieved at the feast of sacred love there is an abundance of spiritual meat remaining. There is always more to follow. Samuel Rutherford could say of the Lord he dearly loved, "He was the ever-running-over Lord Jesus."

A Striking Symbol of Neglect

"Ephraim is a cake not turned." Hosea 7:8.

The prophet Hosea was rich in his use of arrestive symbols to illustrate spiritual truths, and none was so pointed as that of the cake a housewife failed to make thoroughly. The word *thorough* means "through and through." Ephraim was not wholly the Lord's but was like a cake not turned—uncooked on one side and overbaked on the side nearest the fire. Ephraim was not obedient through and through. The people of Ephraim experienced grace, but such grace had not gone to the very center of their being so as to be felt in all thoughts, words, and actions. It is sadly possible to appear holy in one place yet reign in sin in another.

A cake not turned is soon burned on the side nearest the fire, a symbol of one who is "saint in public but a devil in practice. The assumed appearance of superior sanctity frequently accompanies a total absence of all vital godliness," said Spurgeon.

Can we say that we are like a well-baked cake, brown all around, or in other parts thoroughly consistent and sanctified in every part of our being? Spurgeon gave us the following prayer:

> If I am cake burned on one side, and dough on the other,
> O Lord, turn me! Turn my unsanctified nature to the fire
> of Thy love and let it feel the sacred glow, and let my
> burnt side cool a little while I learn my own weakness and
> want of heat when I am removed from Thy heavenly
> flame. Let me not be found a double-minded man, but one
> entirely under the powerful influence of reigning grace;
> for well I know if I am left like a cake unturned, and am
> not on both sides the subject of Thy grace, I must be
> consumed for ever amid everlasting burnings.

Have we not need to pray a similar prayer as followers of him who was holy all through?

The Purest of Human Pleasures

"The Lord God planted a garden." *Genesis 2:8.*

The eminent essayist Francis Bacon was an ardent lover of gardens. He wrote, "God Almighty first planted a Garden; and it is the Purest of Human pleasures." As soon as God created man, he fashioned him a garden for the promotion of his enjoyment of the creator. A garden rests the soul and cheers the heart, and we should pray that in our hearts and lives God Almighty may find a garden of his own planting where he can talk with us in the cool of the day. The Bible lover will find much inspiration in what the scripture says about gardens and their flowers and fruits. The first home of the first man was a garden, but there are sad reminiscences in this history of Bible gardens. On a tombstone in a Welsh churchyard this epitaph is found:

> *In a garden the first of our race was deceived:*
> *In a garden the promise of grace was received:*
> *In a garden was Jesus betrayed to His doom;*
> *In a garden His body was laid in a tomb.*

Shakespeare in *Othello* said, "Our bodies are our gardens, to the which our wills are gardeners." If we deem our bodies the temples of the Holy Spirit, then, like watered gardens, they will be full of fragrance rare. Rudyard Kipling's poem "The Glory of the Garden" is superb even though his garden was England. "The Glory of the Garden lies in more than meets the eye," he wrote. He continued:

> *Oh, Adam was a gardener, and God who made him sees*
> *That half a proper gardener's work is done upon his knees,*
> *So when your work is finished, you can wash your hand and pray*
> *For the Glory of the Garden, that it may not pass away!*

The garden of paradise with its twelve kinds of fruit shall never pass away but ever remain for the health of nations.

Enlarge My Life with Multitude of Days

"Be ye also enlarged." *2 Corinthians 6:13.*

Samuel Johnson was somewhat cynical when he wrote the words in the above title, for he went on to say that "life protracted is protracted woe." We who love the Lord who is able to enlarge our steps only want as many days as the Lord can allow us so that our service for him can be lengthened. The Bible has much to say about spiritual enlargement. The carnal Corinthians were static in their spiritual experience, and so Paul exhorted them, "Be ye also enlarged." The apostle assured them, "Our heart is enlarged" or, as the Amplified Bible has it, "O Corinthians, our heart is opened wide, and so pleads, 'Open wide to us also.' "

We need to be enlarged in our knowledge, love, hope, liberality, faith —in every place. God who ever seeks to enlarge our hearts disapproves of contraction in the lives of those who are his. All of his promises warrant enlarged expectations, and he would have us open our hearts as wide as possible to receive all that he is willing to bestow. Because God waits to gratify enlarged, spiritual desires, may our lives exhibit enlargement in prayer, benevolence, pity, and compassion in all our efforts for his glory.

It is essential to guard ourselves against narrow views or feelings, for the heart of God is large; the love of Christ is large; the Gospel commission is large: the provision of mercy is large; and the mansions of Glory are large. I offer this prayer, that we have our narrow hearts enlarged: O Lord, expand my contracted heart, that I may abound in hope, by the power of the Holy Spirit! Thou hast made provision to gratify desires for spiritual enlargement; enable me to open my heart wide to receive all Thou hast for me!

Draw Nearer Me, Sweetly Questioning

"What would ye that I should do for you?" *Mark 10:36.*

Quaint and saintly George Herbert of the early seventeenth century must have had Jesus in mind when he wrote of "quick-ey'd Love" who:

> *Drew nearer to me, sweet questioning*
> *If I lack'd any thing.*

An unidentified writer of the past century left us a most profitable book called *The Master's Questions and His Answers.* Sweetly Jesus questioned the sons of Zebedee, "What would ye that I should do for you?" He could not accede to the request, however, since position in heaven was his Father's decision. To the blind man Jesus met near Jericho, he asked the same question, "What wilt thou that I should do unto thee?" Without hesitation, the beggar said, "That I may receive my sight." Then, sweetly as he questioned, Jesus sweetly answered, "Receive thy sight!" (Luke 18:42).

As we commence each new day, may we hear him ask us what he can do for us as we face the unknown hours ahead, and may we have our petition ready, for if we ask according to his will, he will hear and undertake. "Ask, what shall I give thee?" (1 Kings 3:5). How else can we reply but say, O Lord, grant me victory over inward corruption—purify my heart—make me a vessel of honour, fit for Thy service—impart Thy holiness—write Thy Word on my heart, and enable me to be as a living epistle with Thy precepts written large over my life—fashion me into Thy likeness, and enable me to live for the honour and glory of Thy free and sovereign grace!

Let us ever remember that Jesus is always at his pardon office, sitting on a throne of grace, and always in a gracious and loving temper to give us what we ask of him in reply to his question, "What would you like me to do for you?"

When There's Trouble Brewing

"Trouble is near." *Psalm 22:11.*

When troubles were brewing, Charles Knight, an eighteenth-century English publisher, asked:

> *Are we downhearted?*
> *No! let 'em all come.*

Trouble and the believer, and the unbeliever also, are never long apart. The difference is that the believer, who is never apart from Jesus, is never downhearted when trouble is near. Jesus is always a very *present* help in trouble. Trouble may be used by Satan to make us wander from Jesus, but Jesus will not abandon us.

We certainly live in a troubled world, and hearts fail for fear. But we have the assurance that although troubles may be near, whether personal, national, or international, the throne of grace is near and his promises are at hand to calm and counsel us. God invites us to call upon him in the day of trouble, and he promises to deliver us. In turn we are to honor him. Any kind of trouble, then, is meant to make God more precious to our hearts. He does not permit trouble to come our way in order to fill us with confusion, weaken our faith, and drive us from his loving heart. We have his promise, "I will be with him in trouble" (Ps. 91:15). He is ever near to sanctify our trials, to glorify his grace, to deepen his work within us, to brighten our evidences, and to fill us with joy and peace in believing. Our attitude toward God then determines whether our trouble is a bane or a blessing. As Edmund V. Cooke, who died in 1932, put it:

> *Oh, a trouble's a ton, or a trouble's an ounce,*
> *Or a trouble is what you make it.*
> *And it isn't the fact that you're hurt that counts,*
> *But only, how did you take it?*

Repairer of Broken Earthenware

"A heart broken and crushed, O God Thou wilt not despise." *Psalm 51:17*, ASB.

Several years ago Harold Begbie, a gifted writer and an ardent admirer of the work of the Salvation Army, wrote a moving book he called *Broken Earthenware*. In it he described the stories of men and women whose hearts and lives had been broken and crushed by sin but who had been transformed by God through the ministry of the army. Our world today is full of broken earthenware, those brokenhearted people who through one cause or another will end their days crushed and destroyed. In "A Jacobite's Epitaph" Thomas Macaulay referred to them: "O'er English dust. A broken heart lies here."

The Bible, a faithful mirror of human life, has much to say about broken hearts and about the causes of such crushing grief. Jeremiah, the weeping prophet, reflected this sorrow of God when he cried, "Mine heart within me is broken because of the prophets . . . and because the land is full of adulterers" (Jer. 23:9).

Do the apostasy and adultery of our time move our hearts as deeply? Do rivers of tears run down our faces because of a powerless religion and a corrupt society? It is said that reproach broke Jesus' heart and that because he literally died of a broken heart, as evidenced by the blood and water from his pierced side, he is able to heal the brokenhearted. How poignant is the lament of Paul over the effort of friends to deter him from his task: "What mean ye to weep and to break mine heart?" Solomon said that through "sorrow of the heart the spirit is broken" (Prov. 15:13). Is yours a broken spirit? Are you, either through your own mistakes or the action of others, broken and crushed? Then claim the promise, The Lord is near to the brokenhearted, and saves those who are crushed in spirit. He alone can mend broken hearts and lives. As Oscar Wilde expressed it in "The Ballad of Reading Gaol":

> How else but through a broken-heart,
> May the Lord Christ enter in?

A Bundle of Contradictions

"As having nothing, and yet possessing all things."
2 Corinthians 6:10.

C. Caleb Cotton, essayist of the early eighteenth century, wrote that "man is an embodied paradox, a bundle of contradictions." But the Bible possesses many embodied paradoxes and is a bundle of seeming contradictions. The above assertion of Paul is one of them. How can we be poor if rich? These blessed contradictions are worthy of our study.

The majority of the Lord's family are not materially rich but generally poor, and the world around may look at them as having nothing valuable or calculated to make them content and happy. But how wrong they are. The poorest saints are heirs of God, having him as their portion and inheritance. While they do not have much of the world's wealth, theirs is the gold tried in the fire, making them spiritually rich. Would that we could be found possessing all the things we have in the Lord. He is our never-failing treasury, and James Smith, a British writer, reminded us in *Daily Remembranceer*, of what we have in him:

> His eternity as the date of our happiness; His
> unchangeableness, the rock of our rest; His omnipotence,
> our constant guard; His faithfulness, our daily security;
> His mercies, our overflowing store; His omniscience, our
> careful overseer; His wisdom, our judicious Counsellor;
> His justice, our stern avenger; His omnipresence, our
> sweet company; His holiness, the fountain from which we
> receive sanctifying grace; His all-sufficiency, the lot
> of our inheritance; His infinity, the extent of our
> glorious portion.

Beloved, if we have little of this world's goods, we have a marvelous fortune at our disposal in God who waits to give us all he has, richly to enjoy. Ours is the privilege of living as heirs of heaven, poor yet rich; unknown by the world as heirs of eternal wealth, ye are yet fully known to him who is owner of all. Though poor, we can make many rich, said Paul who owned little more than the clothes he wore.

To Business That We Love We Rise Betime

"I must be about my Father's business." *Luke 2:49.*

How appropriate are the lines of Shakespeare in *Antony and Cleopatra* in respect to Christ's constant endeavor to finish the work his Father had given him to do:

> *To business that we love we rise betime*
> *And go to't with delight.*

The Son delighted to do the will of his Father and would often rise betime to converse with his Father about the business he had entrusted to him. Literally, the word Christ used for business means "affairs" or "the things of my Father." The Revised Version reads, "Knew ye not that I must be in My Father's House?" (Luke 2:49). These are his first recorded words and, although uttered when he was but a twelve-year-old lad, indicate that he knew at that very early age his purpose in the world.

This first saying of his is significant also because it gives us the key to the whole of his life and mission. Bible teacher and writer G. Campbell Morgan, who died in 1945, commented, "The compelling force, the *must* behind all His doing and teaching, was ever the same: the things of His Father. He lived and wrought only to do the will of God."

We are happy parents if our children relate their lives to God by the *must* of complete surrender to his will. Are we found doing the King's business, not only with haste, but with delight? Are we being borne along by the Master's compelling force to finish the task the Father has allotted us? The majority around us have no idea why they are in the world, and having never discovered the divine plan for their lives, they drift with the tide. But if we are the Lord's, then no matter what legitimate business is ours whereby we can work to live, the Father's business must always have our sincere attention. His affairs should be our chief concern.

To Know That You Know Not

"I know not how." . . . "The Lord knoweth how."
1 Kings 3:7; 2 Peter 2:9.

Francis Bacon in one of his great essays said, "If you dissemble sometimes your knowledge of that you are thought to know, you shall be thought, another time, to know what you know not." With all our acquired and assumed knowledge there are many things we know not. "We know not what a day may bring forth" (Jas. 4:14, free trans.). When Solomon succeeded his father David as king, he was clothed with all humility and confessed, "I am but a little child! I know not how to go out or come in" (1 Kings 3:7). God had said to him, "Ask what I shall give thee" (1 Kings 3:5), and Solomon asked for an understanding heart and discernment of character.

We know not the way we should take in many decisions that have to be made, but God knows the way we must take; and when he has tried us, we come forth as gold. Job's great triumph of faith can be ours if we have learned to sing with an unidentified writer, "In every hour, in perfect peace, I'll sing, He knows! He knows!"

We do not know how to face the burdens of tomorrow, but do we need to know? Is not today's burden enough, and has not God said, "As thy day, so shall thy strength be" (Deut. 33:25)? Why then add tomorrow's load to today's? If you feel tomorrow's burden will crush, let it happen tomorrow and not today. The Lord knows how to deliver the godly out of the trials awaiting them. We know not how we are to meet this problem, situation, choice, or sorrow, but the Lord knows how; and as we rest in him, he makes our way plain. Perhaps you have recently been bereaved and are saying to your heart, "I know not how I am to face the coming days without the loved one who was so much a part of my life." But God knows how you will fare, for he has made every provision for the vacant place in your heart and home. So why not leave tomorrow in the hands of him who said, "Let the morrow take thought for itself" (Matt. 6:34).

Death Is Entrance into Light

"Seek him that . . . turneth the shadow of death into the morning." *Amos 5:8.*

Our descriptions of death are as somber as the event itself. We speak of "death's dark night," "the terrors of death," "the icy hand of death," "death, the least of all evils." But the declaration of Amos is that God turns the shadow into substance, night into morning. Samuel Johnson in his satiric verse *The Vanity of Human Wishes* said:

> *Faith, that, panting for a happier seat,*
> *Counts death kind Nature's signal of retreat.*

Faith in God enables us to count death as the signal of retreat from the dark shadows of this world into the glorious abode above. Death is the passage way from the mortal into the immortal. During World War II a sincere Christian soldier whose name is unknown was instantly killed in battle, but some time before his death he had set forth his conception of leaving earth for glory in the following poem:

> *Best loved of all I leave behind. I see*
> *O Heaven, pity those who cannot see!*
> *Glory on glory—glory on that face*
> *So near, so dear; gold glory on the wave,*
> *Purple and gold and darting tongues of flame;*
> *Calm glory on the cloud-piled dome of heaven;*
> *Glory of fire on the earth's great face.*
> *So slips my soul, scarce heeding of the change,*
> *From glory unto glory! Heaven breaks*
> *Eternal glory, on the face of God!*

Christ's death and resurrection have given us the assurance that in him only the shadow of death will be transformed for us into glory unspeakable.

Transmuted in the Furnace of Affliction

"When he hath tried me, I shall come forth as gold."
Job 23:10.

The experiences and utterances of Job, which the New Testament presents as a model of patience, are a mixture of confidence and complaint. In the chapter before us, in the midst of Job's bitter complaining and sighing after God, there flames forth a most remarkable evidence of the tenacity of his faith. He was confident that God was behind his trials and through all the processes of testing was seeking the vindication of the true gold in his servant. In the furnace of affliction the divine goldsmith was transmuting Job's life into a most precious vessel. Malachi assured us that God sits as the refiner and purifier of silver.

Dr. Robert G. Lee, master of words whose eloquent preaching often thrilled me, commented on Job's assertion:

> The fire of the furnace and the smoke of the flames—
> these show how God brings deep things out of the dark—
> rich treasures out of darkness. Authorities tell us that the
> potter never sees his clay take on rich shades of silver,
> or red, or cream, or brown, until after the darkness and the
> burning of the furnace. These colors come—after the
> burning and darkness. The clay is beautiful—the vase is
> made possible—after the burning and darkness. How
> wide-lying and universal is this law of life! When did the
> bravest man and purest woman you know get their
> whitened characters? Did they not get them as the clay
> gets its beauty and glory—after the darkness and burning
> of the furnace?

It may be that you are presently being sorely tried and are mystified by what God is permitting to overtake you. Remember that he dwells in "thick darkness" as well as in light and is with you in the darkness of your furnace, trying you, sifting out the dross, and transmuting your life into a golden vessel more fit for his use.

He That Is Down Need Fear No Fall

"God resisted the proud, but giveth grace unto the humble." *James 4:6.*

In his Sermon on the Mount Jesus called those who were humble "poor in spirit." He did not mean, however, that they were poor-spirited. He meant that they were conscious that their own righteousness was but filthy rags in the presence of a thrice-holy God and that their own fleshy wisdom was but folly to Him. Only those who do not shun the valley of humiliation prove it to be a place of hope. Only as we learn of our own poverty and ignorance are we ready to learn of God and to trust him.

Contrary to worldly policy, humility is the root of all progress in knowledge and of all dependence on God from which his bounty springs. Some of the greatest persons in knowledge or personality are generally the most humble. Sir James Simpson of Edinburgh, discoverer of chloroform, was once asked what he deemed his greatest discovery. This was his quick reply: "That I was a sinner, and that Christ died for me!" Knowledge with such persons enables them to realize how little they know.

All who are the Lord's should seek to adorn the garment of true humility, for such a virtue is the basis of further virtues such as a quiet mind, gratitude, contentment, and, above all, robust faith in God's ability to undertake for us in any circumstances of life. The consistent teaching of him who was "meek and lowly in heart" was that the gates of the kingdom of God are ever open to the lowly hearted and to those who knew that there is nothing between them and great darkness, now and beyond, but the pity of God. Thomas à Kempis has taught us to pray, "Surely my heart cannot rest, nor be entirely contented, unless it rest in Thee, and rise above all gifts and all creatures whatsoever." Only as we realize that we are nothing, have nothing, and can do nothing apart from God can we be graced with the humility which James declared to be God's gift.

There Was No Leaf upon the Forest Bare

"He hath stripped me." *Job 19:9.*

In a most poignant way Job told us how God had denuded him of his glory, his crown, his honor, his children, his familiar friends, his possessions and position, leaving him as a barren tree. As I write this meditation, I glance out of my study window and gaze for a moment at several trees near my garden. During the summer their foliage was abundant and beautiful, but there they stand gaunt, bare, leafless. Stripped of all their glory, they are not a pleasant sight to behold. This was how Job felt in his wretched and lonely condition. In his own epitaph Benjamin Franklin spoke of his corpse as "the cover of an old book with contents worn out and *stript of its letting and gilding—food for worms.*" Death is indeed the final stripper.

Does your life seem desolate and bare, a leafless tree? Perhaps you have been stripped of all that made life worth living. A dear one, so precious to your heart and upon who you were so dependent, was taken from you, and in that one's death your own heart seems to have died. Now you stand on the bleak summit of your deep grief, no longer sheltered by the one long loved but lost awhile, stripped like a tree of all its summer dress and beauty.

Well, you must not yield to despair but live in hope that, as a tree planted by the Lord in his garden, you will blossom again and no longer stand as a naked tree. Job lost all in his trials but lived to see the day when God gave him back twice as much as he had lost, with his latter end being more richly blessed than his beginning. Above all, think of Jesus who was stripped of all and died naked on a leafless tree but who is now clothed and crowned with honor and glory.

Under His Wings I Am Safely Abiding

"Cover thee with his feathers . . . his wings." *Psalm 91:4.*

The dominant feature of this great psalm, ascribed to Moses, the man of God, is that of the security of one whose whole trust is in the Lord. The Book of Common Prayer puts the verse as, "He shall defend thee under his wings, and thou shalt be safe under His feathers." How precious is the illustration Jesus used of himself as a hen yearning to shelter her chicks under her warm feathers! The psalm before us, rich in its singular personal pronouns, is fragrant with the satisfaction of the heart that has God as its dwelling place. The psalmist referred to this habitation as "the secret place," and described its complete security by employing the figure of the mother-bird to illustrate "The shadow of the Almighty" (91:1).

As we read this psalm, we must not forget that the safety offered is of a spiritual nature rather than a material experience. As those redeemed by the precious blood of Christ, we are not always immune from physical plagues and pains. "Many are the afflictions of the righteous" (Ps. 34:19). The truth conveyed by promises of security is that the saints are ever guarded from destructive spiritual forces as they dwell in the secret place of the Most High; only through Christ are they admitted to the most intimate fellowship with God. Our life is hid with Christ in God. In Jesus who came as the shadow of the Almighty we are privileged to dwell, now and forever, in the secret place with its eternal safety. William O. Cushing's chorus rings out to each of us:

> *Under His wings, under His wings,*
> *Who from His love can sever?*
> *Under His wings my soul shall abide,*
> *Safely abide for ever.*

The Handkerchief of the Lord

"He maketh the grass to grow." *Psalm 147:8.*

The splendor of grass is beautifully set forth in the lines from "Songs of Myself" from *Leaves of Grass* by Walt Whitman, who died in 1892:

A child said What is the grass? *fetching it to me with full hands,* . . .
. . . I guess it is the handkerchief of the Lord,
A scented gift and remembrance designedly dropt,
Bearing the owner's name someway in the corners,
*   that we may see and remark, and say* Whose?

As we clothe our children with attractive and beneficial garments, so, said Jesus, God clothes the fields with lovely grass of various kinds. The psalmist told us that "God causeth the grass to grow for the cattle" (104:14). How could they, or we, although human, exist without it? Where would our milk, butter, cheese, and wool come from if it were not for the grass? Grass is not only for our provision but for our pleasure, for there is nothing more pleasing to the eye than the beautiful green covering the earth like a carpet.

If God so clothes the earth with grass, surely he will not fail to take care of us, as Jesus clearly taught in his illustration of the grass of the field. The psalmist has a further reference to grass: "God maketh the grass to grow upon mountains" (147:8), meaning in the least likely and the most difficult places. The word *maketh* reminds us that the power of God is under the root of the grass, causing it to grow even in shallow soil that is never nurtured. If life for us is not in some sheltered valley but exposed in a most difficult sphere, is it not encouraging to know that God can enable us to grow in grace and in the knowledge of him in the least likely place? Having charmed us with the color of grass, he is able to make us pleasing in his sight—and in the sight of others.

A Most Profitable Exercise

"It is a good thing to give thanks unto the Lord."
Psalm 92:1.

The phrase arresting our attention is this advice from the Hebrew saint, "It is a good thing." Profit in praise was a high expression of approval and took the psalmist back to the first divine approval recorded in the Bible—"God saw the light, that it was good." At creation each divine feat found adequate expression in the repeated word *good*. This highest word of approval God had for his own works is used here by the psalmist. Praise to God is "a good thing" because it is in harmony with the original design of creation. Although sin brought discord into the world, God made all things harmonious, and the response of an unfallen world was in song—"The morning stars sang together, and all the sons of God shouted for joy" (Job 38:7). Is it not a good thing to emulate the divine ideal of things and add to the world's harmonies and not to its discords?

Good to give. Life is enriched in its noblest aspects by giving rather than by constant receiving. It is a good thing when we learn to give.

Good to give thanks. What grander or better virtue is there than appreciating the source of goodness, its value, and the acknowledgment of our own indebtedness. Those who never give thanks miss one of the essential attributes of human nature, namely, gratitude.

Good to give thanks unto the Lord. He is a constant and bountiful giver, and in our thanks to him we give something back, particularly if we offer the sacrifice of praise. Giving thanks is therefore a good thing because it imparts joy to the heart of the Lord himself. No song in God's world that is pure and unselfish fails to reach his ear. As he yearns for our *Thank you!* it must ever be a good thing to rejoice the heart of him from whom all blessings flow. We are urged "to sing praise unto Thy name" (Ps. 92:1). It is a good thing when gratitude melts into song and we find ourselves singing unto the Lord who ever hears "the robins sing on earth."

Thy Kind but Searching Glance

"Examine me . . . prove me . . . try me." Psalm 26:2.

Examinations as a rule are not pleasant experiences. Young people dread them at school. Searchings of our persons and possessions for security reasons at airports are inconvenient but not to be feared if we have nothing to hide. David asked God, a very keen and thorough examiner, to search his life for any hidden sin or weakness. He wanted everything known to God to be made known to himself. David sought heaven's vindication of his character. Desiring no wicked way to remain within his heart, the psalmist used three words: *examine, prove, try*. The Amplified Bible presents the passage, "Examine me, O Lord, and try me; Test my heart and my mind."

These are forcible words. *Examine* implies a fiery process, a burning up of all dross, leaving behind only that which can pass through the fire. *Try, prove,* and *test* are likewise expressive; the Hebrew words mean a melting by fire. Thus David prayed for a searching by fire—a symbol of the Holy Spirit—that should burn up all that was contrary to the will of God.

Failure in school examinations often creates a determination never to fail again and is therefore profitable. David felt that if God examined him thoroughly, sin and ignorance would be revealed, and when they were removed, his life would be more fit for God to use. It is encouraging to know that the divine searcher is our loving heavenly Father whose kind but searching glance scans the very wounds that shame would hide in order to heal them. Paul urged the Corinthians to *examine* themselves as to whether they were *in* the faith. It is sadly possible to work *for* the faith yet not be *in* it. Self-introspection can result in despair. It is far better to pray with David, "Search me, O Lord!" He knows how to throw light into the darkened cells until conscience feels the loathsomeness of sin. And, blessed be his name, what his search reveals, his blood can cleanse.

Taking True for False, or False for True

"Old shoes and clouted upon their feet." Joshua 9:5.

Tennyson, in *Idylls of the King*, described a "race of miserable men" who:

> *Do forge a lifelong trouble for ourselves,*
> *By taking true for false, or false for true.*

Joshua had to face a good deal of trouble as the result of taking the false for true in his encounter with the deceiving Gibeonites who came with the intent of misleading the wise leader of Israel and cleverly succeeded. The Book of Common Prayer has a supplication for deliverance from "blasphemous fables, and dangerous deceits." Evidently Joshua did not offer such a petition. He was beguiled by the wily Gibeonites with their tattered clothes, worn-out shoes, and moldy bread because he "did not ask counsel at the mouth of the Lord" (Josh. 9:14). Famous for his stratagem as leader of Israel's forces, yet because he acted on his own as he listened to the fabricated story of the Gibeonites, he was found wanting in keen discernment.

Hypocrites fall into two classes. Some profess to be better than they are, and these form a large group. Others profess to be worse than they are or poorer than they are. The Gibeonites were of this latter class. They acted as if they were very poor, not only to gain sympathy, but to save their necks from death. These deceivers likely had large wardrobes, wealthy homes, and plenty of good food.

One lesson we can learn from them is never to act what we are not. May we be saved from all deceitfulness in righteousness. A sign of the last times is the way multitudes will believe a lie, even as, alas, Joshua did. Satan is the archdeceiver who beguiled Eve through his subtlety and who, although the fiend of darkness, can transform himself into an angel of light. Our protection against satanic wiles is the constant effort to seek counsel of the Lord, praying that spiritual intuition may be ours to detect immediately that which is not of the Lord.

To Measure Life Learn Thou Betimes

"He that spake with me had for a measure a golden reed
to measure the city." *Revelation 21:15*, RV.

Measures meet us at every turn of the avenue. One wonders if we could exist without measure for many phases of life. The house you live in represents precise measuring. The clothes you wear were made by measure. The food you eat comes in measured form. The light and gas you use come to you through the *meter*, a word meaning "that which measures." The roads you walk on required a good deal of measuring. The laws of the land charges as unlawful the tampering with recognized measurements. All standards of measurement must be maintained accurately and beyond all suspicion.

The Lord is the one with the measuring rod who tests your life and mine to see if it conforms to his standard measurement. The Bible is God's law from heaven for our life on earth and presents Jesus as one infallible standard. Paul prayed for grace to measure up to the stature of the perfect man in Jesus, who had a good deal to say about measures and measuring.

As cities and towns are subjected to endless measurements in their creation, so the Holy City, the heavenly Jerusalem, indicates perfect planning. Precise measuring is found in the details: "The city lieth foursquare" and was measured out by one with his "golden reed" (Rev. 21:15, 16). (A reed from the hedge was the first measure people used.)

One apparent lesson we learn from all this is that God wills us to order our lives systematically, conforming to his standards. Long ago people measured with their thumbs—an inch being the distance between the knuckle and the first joint. This became known as the "rule of thumb" but was not very exact. God, who measures our days, would not have us plan life in any such haphazard way but by his certain and infallible standard. To bring us up to the divine measurement, we have the power of the Holy Spirit who is given to us without measure.

Good Order Is the Foundation of All Good Things

"Make the men sit down by fifties in a company."
Luke 9:14.

Edmund Burke's principle of "good order" is certainly illustrated in the action of Jesus when he commanded the five thousand to sit down by fifties in a company. Had they rushed upon him, crowding around him in a confused, feverish fashion, he would not have been able to dispense the good things he had to satisfy their hunger. So we read, "And they do so." What a sight! A multitude sitting down in groups of fifty, looking up into the face of the one who was the object of all their hope, who alone knew how to command a well-nigh unmanageable crowd.

Phillips Brooks once preached a powerful sermon on the phrase, "Make the men sit down." He indicated that at that moment all the excitement subsided; instead of the people pushing toward and surging around Jesus, they were made to sit down in readiness to receive from him what he was prepared to give. Brooks went on to show that this action is illustrative of two stages in Christian experience: First, when people rush hurriedly after good things, their religious life is full of excitement and even worry. Second, when they sit down, their restlessness and confusion give way to calm patience and watchful waiting—an essential and important part of spiritual experience.

Christ was ever the master of assemblies and knew how to act in an emergency. He never lost command to make people sit down, and as his followers we should never lose our equanimity in the presence of tumultuous trials and cares. Like Mary, we should always be found sitting at his feet, ready to be fed by him. When we fulfill the Master's commands, we discover that there is always more than enough to satisfy our hunger for the bread he alone can give.

He Sat Him Down in a Lonely Place

"Ye shall . . . leave me alone." John 16:32.

In "The Poet's Song" Tennyson depicts the poet sitting down in a lonely place and chanting a melody loud and sweet:

> *That made the wild-swan pause in her cloud,*
> *And the lark drop down at his feet.*

Jesus, who inspired some of the greatest lines in poetry, knew what it was to sit down often in a lonely place, but although alone, there was ever a sweet melody in his heart, for he could say, "The Father hath not left me alone" (John 8:29).

There is a twofold aspect of the loneliness Jesus predicted we would suffer. First, he was alone as far as his disciples were concerned. In spite of their ecstatic utterances that they would never be offended by what he said or did and would never forsake him no matter who else did, the great purposes of his life and mission were largely hidden from them because they were not able to comprehend them. Certainly, Jesus was not alone in the sense of being without the love, sympathy, and confidence of his disciples. They believed in him, trusted him, and tried to enter into a living sympathy with his sorrows. What they failed to share with Jesus was the divine purpose of his marvelous self-denial even unto death and the offering up of himself as the sole atonement of the world's sins.

Second, Jesus was alone as far as the world was concerned, for it would not have him to reign over it. The world was ever hostile to his claims and rejected his love and grace. Because of our allegiance to him, we may find ourselves sharing his loneliness, but although lonely, we are not alone. Ours is the assurance that Jesus had throughout his sojourn in a lonely place. His Father was his abiding companion and is likewise our confidence. Hug the promise to your heart, lonely witness, "The Father hath not left me alone."

The Sermon a Penny Preached

"Bring me a penny, that I may see it." Mark 12:15.

When we want to emphasize the influence money wields, or "answereth to all things" as Solomon put it, we say, *Money talks*. The small penny in the hand of Jesus certainly did talk although its witness was silent until Jesus gave it a voice in his question. Pointing to Caesar's profile on the Roman coin, Jesus asked, "Whose is this image and superscription?" (Matt. 22:20). Greater in value than our modern penny, the *denarius* Jesus asked for was the principal Roman coin, just as the *drachma*, or "piece of silver" the woman lost, was the principal Greek coin of the day. The miniature piece of silver Jesus asked for bore the name and likeness of the emperor, indicating that he had made it his own and that bearing his superscription he had claim upon it. Distributed among his subjects, such money represented his power and his right to rule.

In a most effective way Jesus told the message of the penny. In reply to his question about the image on it, the people said, "Caesar's." He said, "Render to Caesar the things that are Caesar's; and to God the things that are God's" (Mark 12:17). No wonder the people marveled at the sermon on obligations, heavenward and earthward, that he made the penny preach. The emperor's image was stamped upon silver that had been purified and made ready for use. The question each heart must ask is, Am I as purified silver, fit for the Master's service, and therefore qualified to bear his stamp upon my heart and life?

All who are redeemed by the blood of Jesus are his coinage, and he seeks to use them as his current coin in the world wherever they go. Bearing his image, they are recognized as his property. By their spirit and conduct and by the words they speak and deeds they do, they glorify God as their owner and fulfill in the world all that is legally expected of them, no matter who their governing caesar may be.

If You Were Suddenly to See Me, Could You Recognize Me?

"There standeth one among you, whom ye know not."
John 1:26.

Ovid, the Latin philosopher, affirmed of himself, "Nor, if you were suddenly to see me, could you recognize me." Jesus appeared suddenly to many in the days of his flesh, but they failed to recognize him as the Messiah. When the priests and Levites asked, "*Who* art thou?" he readily confessed, "I am the Christ." But those of his own nationality received him not. That man of vision who heralded Jesus' coming, John the Baptist, had no hesitation in proclaiming that Jesus was the Son of God. Joseph and Mary did not understand why he was in the world, and he rebuked them by affirming, "Wist ye not that I must be about my Father's business?"

One of the mysteries of the ages is the stupidity of human beings, who, although surrounded by natural objects, took thousands of years to discover what God had put close by their side for use. Sorrowfully the Savior of the world lamented, "There standeth one among you"—the supreme fact of life—"whom ye know not"—the supreme folly of life, for to know him is eternal life.

How privileged we are to have God's beloved Son standing among us! His presence is an inspiration, and his grace is sufficient for every need. The tragedy, however, is that so many around us do not know that he is standing at the door waiting for recognition and admission to their hearts as their Savior. It has been said that "the scales of neglect cover the eyes and darken the soul." This statement is true of those who, neglecting the great salvation, fail to see in the Savior the effulgence of the Father's glory and the express image of his person. How blessed you are if with Paul you can say, "I know whom [not what] I have believed (2 Tim. 1:12), and have the assurance that life everlasting is yours through knowing him!

As Straight As a Die

"The Lord said unto me, Amos, what seest thou? And
I said, A plumbline." *Amos 7:8.*

In one of his books Arnold Bennett described Half Bursley as having a grudge against Ralph "because he's as straight as a die, and always knows what he wants, and is always clever enough to get . . . . People don't like it—naturally." Those who strive to see the crooked made straight are not popular in a crooked world. The purpose of the plumbline the Lord showed Amos was to see that a wall went up perfectly straight. While the modern spirit level is now widely used, bricklayers still place the plumbline against the wall as it is being built to test whether it is perfectly perpendicular.

In a way, Israel had been built up as a nation with a plumbline, and everything being right, God approved of his people. But they fell into the crooked ways of idolatry, and Amos was raised up to warn King Jeroboam, the high priest, and the nation of their departure from the straight road. Tested by the divine plumbline, the people were upright no longer. God's wall, so gloriously built, was no longer perpendicular, and grieved with the departure from his ways, he declared that he would take it down to the foundation.

As with nations of antiquity, so with ourselves. God is ever using his perfect plumbline, namely, the grand old Book by which lives are tried, to see if the building of life and character is according to his plan. The Bible is our law from heaven for life on this earth, and we are wise if we always test our motives and desires by this infallible plumbline which God is ever placing alongside our conduct to see whether it is according to his rule. If there are bulging defects, then we are not to be discouraged, for the one with the plumbline in his hand is able to make crooked things straight.

Give Me the Splendid Silent Sun

"For the Lord God is a sun." Psalm 84:11.

"Give me the splendid silent sun with all his beams full-dazzling." This phrase of Walt Whitman's can be used of our Lord. Among the many types or symbols the Lord uses of himself, this one—a sun—is the most compelling. This earth cannot exist without the sun, bright and shining in the heavens, and what the sun is to the world, the Lord is to its inhabitants. In some mysterious way the world is kept in place by the attraction of the sun which exerts a mighty power as the center of earth's system. Thus the earth goes around its orbit and never wanders from its path. As the sun keeps the earth in place, so the Lord, by his attractive power, keeps us in the orbit of his will.

Among the benefits of the sun is *light*. How dull the day is when the sunbeams are not dazzling! There is beauty all around when the sun shines. As the light and heat of the sun are everything to the fields and gardens, so the Lord, as a sun, is the light of the world, banishing its spiritual darkness. When he appears as the sun of righteousness with healing in his wings, the gloom of earth will disappear.

But the sun not only provides us with light; it is also the source of *life*. Invalids have been restored to health by basking in the sun. Plants in the garden, deadlike through the winter, live again as the kindly sun shines on them when summer approaches. Similarly, the Lord as a sun is the source of life, and we live anew when we turn our hearts and faces toward him in penitence and faith. If the Lord God is the sun in the universe of your heart, then may grace be yours to walk in his light and love.

The Murmuring of Innumerable Bees

"They compassed me about like bees." Psalm 118:12.

"Sweet is every sound" and "every soul is sweet," said Tennyson, and among these sweet sounds the poet included "the murmuring of innumerable bees." To those who are afraid of bees, their buzzing is not a very sweet sound. In a well-flowered garden bees often surround one, but as a rule they only compass about those who threaten to attack their hives and rob them of the little treasure they have been accumulating for many busy months to sustain their lives during the hard winter. Bees seem to know their enemies as well as their friends and usually do not sting unless there is a cause.

Are there some ways in which we can imitate the busy bee? I think so. We cannot blame bees in the least for compassing about those who set out to rob them of their possessions. Do not tricksters who live by plundering the hard earnings of others deserve to be stung? The skill bees exhibit in building is superb. The hive, or home, is unique in intricacy, ingenuity, and utility. Beauty and order are conspicuous—a less for us to give of our very best, not only in what our hands find to do, but in our service for God. Even clever bees are not perfect, for there are drones among them, just as there are among humans.

Are you among the *busy* bees? In a hive nurse-bees move about softly, caring for the sick and the newborn. In God's family there is need and room for more nurse-bees. Conspicuous among bees' activities is the way they store up food for the future. Cells are filled with honey and then sealed until winter comes and there is urgent need of food. Too often we live only for the present, heedless of preparing for coming days. What folly is ours when we neglect to provide, not only for our future here, but for eternity beyond this vale of tears. Some bees go out to work; some stay at home caring for others, but all share alike. "As his part is that goeth down to the battle, so shall his part be that tarrieth by the stuff: they shall part alike" (1 Sam. 30:24).

Thy Stained Name—from All Stains Free

"Can any good thing come out of Nazareth?" John 1:46.

The above question was asked by Nathanael, an inhabitant of a neighboring village who evidently looked upon Nazareth with something of local jealousy and scorn. The form of his question also suggests an ill repute in reference to those who lived there. At the outset let it be made clear that to be called a *Nazarene* was altogether different from being known as a *Nazarite*, a Hebrew under the vow of abstinence. Jesus was a true Nazarite and also a Nazarene—a term equivalent to shame and contempt. He was brought up in Nazareth and was known as "Jesus the Nazarene."

Sneeringly, Nathanael asked, "Can any good thing come out of such a despicable town?" Jesus came out of it, and he was "holy, harmless, undefiled, and separate from sinners." Over his mangled form on the cross they wrote, "Jesus of Nazareth." And as a true Nazarene, he stooped to the lowest depths of ignominy on our behalf. For our salvation he was willing to endure hatred and contempt. Nazareth, however, lost its stain through Christ's contact with the place. He is the cruse of salt flavoring every bitter spring of life. To quote from an unknown writer:

> *Though a name of evil holding*
> *There was brought the Undefiled.*
> *Like a dove, a serpent folding,*
> *There grew up the Hold Child.*
> Nazareth! *Cross-like we see*
> *Thy stained name, from all stains free.*

115

Contempt, Farewell! And Maiden Pride, Adieu!

"Take heed, that you despise not one of the little ones."
Matthew 18:10.

The Master's warning against the danger of contempt was uttered when the disciples were wrangling for the foremost place in his kingdom. Their pride prevented them from taking a lowly place. The words in the title above, from Shakespeare's *Much Ado About Nothing*, continue: "No glory lives behind the back of such" contempt and pride. The only person fit for the kingdom of heaven is the humblest. The disciples were not childlike, and they were in peril of the contempt accompanying pride. In the New Testament the word *despise* which Jesus used is only once found in a neutral sense and once in a commendable sense. In every other reference it is cast in reproach. The favorable and only exception is that describing Jesus as "despising the shame" (Heb. 12:2). "Take heed that ye *despise* not" (Matt. 18:10).

Scripture is against cherishing contempt toward anything or anybody. Flourishing in an atmosphere of pride, the spirit of contempt is always impoverishing to those who possess it. The word *despise* itself means to "think down upon" or "look down on one." When a person "thinks down upon" others, he or she thinks of them from the exalted position created in his or her own imagination.

Jesus told his disciples not to think down upon the little ones before him but to be clothed with humility. How much more forcible is the warning of Jesus when applied to those who, in the spirit of pride, belittle others! Contempt toward those nobler than they are earns divine condemnation. In fact, said Jesus, they are not godlike since they despise what the Father in heaven values greatly. To the extent that we despise anyone who is humble, we are unlike the Father. Further, we are unlike the angels who guard the little ones if we despise them. Courtiers of heaven, the angels are ever near to those who are childlike in heart and action. May ours be the spirit of the Master himself who was ever meek and lowly in heart.